DA BROOKLYN
I REMEMBA

Written by
Leonard M. De Virgilio
&
Sophia Vailakis-De Virgilio

TABLE OF CONTENTS

DEDICATIONS

TO: MY GRANDPARENTS, AND MY MOTHER AND FATHER, FROM WHOM I LEARNED SO MUCH WITHOUT THEM SAYING A WORD TO ME.

MY KIDS; LOUISE, JOSEPH AND ELI, FOR WHOM I HAVE EVERLASTING LOVE.

MY GRANDSON LUCA, YOU'RE MY HEART AND SOUL. I CAN'T TELL YOU HOW MUCH I LOVE YOU. REACH FOR THE STARS MY BOY! --LOVE, POP-POP

MY SISTER AND MY BROTHER; WE'VE BEEN THROUGH A LOT.

MY WIFE SOPHIA, WHO PUTS UP WITH ALL MY IDIOSYNCRASIES (AND I HAVE LOTS!). ONE OF THE BIGGEST HELPS SHE IS TO ME IS WITH TECHNOLOGY (SHE SOMETIMES CALLS ME A LUDDITE, NOT LIKE HER BUDDY AT WORK, ARAMIS).

MY GODFATHER MICHAEL, WHO NEVER FORSOOK ME AND FOR WHOM I HAVE EVERLASTING LOVE.

MY AUNT EMILY, MY GODMOTHER, YOU NEVER WAVERED WITH YOUR LOVE AND LOYALTY FOR ME. FROM DECEMBER 1950 UNTIL JANUARY 2021.

MY AUNTS AND UNCLES WHO PUT UP WITH ME, AND WERE ALWAYS THERE FOR ME.

THE MUSIC OF DEAN MARTIN, FRANK SINATRA, BOBBY DARIN AND BUDDY HOLLY. ENZO TOGNIERI, MY SECOND FATHER.

FATHER ARTHUR, WHO WAS TOUGHER THAN US.

ALL THE NUNS AND PRIESTS FROM MY CATHOLIC GRAMMAR SCHOOL, WHO WERE LONG ON DISCIPLINE AND SHORT ON COMPASSION.

MY NEIGHBORHOOD, THAT MADE ME THE PERSON I AM TODAY.

P.S. I KNOW THERE ARE A LOT OF DEDICATIONS, BUT I DIDN'T GO THROUGH THIS JOURNEY ALONE.

FORWARD

Preserving Street History

The author's wife and co-author offers the following, and although it may be a little long, it really needs to be said.

We offer this work without apology to describe life from a bye-gone era as told by a man who is hard-working, well-educated, and can still summon the memories of the days when thinking too much about consequences were at the very least discouraged, and in the worst cases, could result in a really bad outcome, but straight-forward in many ways. A multi-layered remembrance of "The School of Hard Knocks" (which would be considered brutality now), the street history, and what it was like growing up in an Italian-American ghetto while still feeling favored. It is also a love letter to the world within the Borough of Brooklyn where Lenny De Virgilio came from, written from the perspectives of a young boy, a pre-teen and young teen. The voice of this author is important to preserve because it may not be widely heard otherwise, if at all in today's world and represents the every-man, the every-woman and the regular Joes and Janes. A perspective that is shunned in many circles, completely dismissed out of hand and even discarded because it can be viewed in a less than generous light, but it represents so many people who are plain-spoken and without airs or the sophistication of the literati. The stories of people who in many cases did not have the benefit of education past grammar school – (kindergarten through 8th grade, now called elementary school, or early education), were working class without much exposure beyond the confines of this enclave, the people who populated South Brooklyn and those like them were the elders for many of us. It's like one of his friends (an Irishman I might add!) said some years ago, as he pointed out, "Why should I leave Court Street? There's the bar, the bread store, the Italian store (the Italian specialty food store, also called the 'pork store') and the video store (pre-streaming), all within a block or two of each other." These

1

simple pleasures are what made our Irish-American friend happy; we love him for it and may God bless him!

The neighborhood of South Brooklyn was one of the many ethnic communities all over New York City, where certain nationalities were concentrated into a geographic area in a practice known as red-lining, often resulting in ethnic ghettos. (Red-lining was the basis used to deny credit-worthy applicants loans, as well as providing other obstacles to prevent them from buying homes, especially outside of their ethnic communities. The effects of these now illegal practices are especially evident within the New York City public school system.) The impact of coming from this ghetto runs deep for all who share this origin, but not necessarily just in the ways you might think. So it's no surprise that despite having an education and exposure to other cultures, the author, Lenny, remains blue-collar in his heart and lifestyle.

Lenny D. has since boyhood, moved halfway across the country for nearly a decade from his South Brooklyn origin and traveled elsewhere in the U.S. as well as abroad. He has had the privilege of mentoring many young people of all stripes through coaching different sports and as a high school teacher of physical education, health and swimming. Mr. D., Coach D. or Mr. Lenny has benefited as much, if not more so than those he was fortunate enough to have in his charge. As a swim coach for an elite high school in Brooklyn, he turned no prospective swimmers away, even kids who needed more basic instruction. One boy on this team had the heart of a lion, really stands out. He was at every practice on time, if not early, working just a little harder than all the other swimmers on the team, but his skills weren't quite there. In one meet, he swam into another lane and should have been disqualified (DQed), but Coach D. spoke to the official and they gave the boy a second try. The whole team was a family, and they rallied around this young man's effort until he finished his heat! At the end of the swim season, at their annual dinner, this student got the "Hold The Rope" award, which Coach D. gave to the person who if you were ever hanging off the side of a mountain and needed someone to pull you up by a rope, this is the person you would choose and I couldn't agree more.

(If you want to understand more about what it means to "hold the rope," have a look at this link:

https://coachfore.org/2012/07/22/hold-the-rope-powerful-and-inspirational-story-for-your-team/)

This was early on in Coach D.'s coaching career and when he developed the official motto for the team of "No excuses, just results." Unofficially, it was "win without abuse, lose without alibi" to give you an idea of the kind of influence Coach D. puts forth. More than a decade later, Coach D. got a private message on Facebook from this 'Hold the Rope' recipient who said that when things weren't going well for him, he would pull out his high school swim t-shirt to look at the motto – "no excuses, just results." This was one of the things that got him through the tough times. Coach D. replied back to ask the young man what he was doing and it turned out he was involved with cancer research for Sloan-Kettering. What an incredible example of the impact one person can have, even coming from such humble beginnings! That was confirmation the right person got that award, but we never doubted it.

For more understanding of the life-shaping experiences of Lenny D., he lost thirteen relatives through gun violence (six male members, one was in the process of committing a crime) or drugs/drinking (one male and three female members). And in one of Lenny's first childhood memories in August of 1958, his best friend and cousin Michael, "Poochie," died on his very first bike ride on 3rd Avenue and President Street. The five-year-old boy was rammed twice against a wall by someone just learning to drive who thought he was hitting the brake but instead fatally crushed the little boy. Fifty feet from where Poochie was killed, Lenny's other cousin Louie was also hit by a car breaking every bone in his body except his pinky, which of course, killed him too. These were formative and haunting events, to say the least.

The most profound takeaway for me in the more than twenty-five years that this man and I have been together was when I threw him his 50th birthday party a few months into our relationship. It was my first look at how things in South Brooklyn worked. He had and still has maybe a few dozen, really close lifelong friends from "the neighborhood," whereas, in contrast, most people are lucky if they can count on one finger, never mind on one hand, the number of close friends they can reliably count. Despite the party venue being able to accommodate 150 people, we invited about 225 to 250 people because of family *and friends* who could NOT be left off the invitation list. People kept calling us to be sure they or someone else were invited, so we just left it to the guests to cycle in and out of the party space hoping not to be overcrowded, and it worked! At the time, I thought to myself (I never said it out loud to him) that the rude awakening we all get in early adulthood about who your "real" friends are, has taken really long to hit him, because all these unwavering friendships was something beyond my comprehension: I didn't believe they were for real! You have to understand, I grew up in a different part of Brooklyn than my husband: each area back then had unique personalities, almost like they were each a different country and giving us our own views on things. And probably not until we began this book endeavor did it really sink in to my thick skull that the unintended outcome of the Lenny's family being shoe-horned/red-lined into that Italian ghetto of South Brooklyn was how deep the bond they had with each other was… it didn't hurt that a good many of them were also related to each other. The author quotes a friend who was not from South Brooklyn and said, "If you had a fight with one person in your neighborhood, you had to fight everyone!" Lenny agreed saying, "Yeah, because we were all related!" Our Super-Storm-Sandy-ravaged little town in Queens and specifically our block, is as close to the South Brooklyn neighborhood of old as you can get. None of our neighbors are related to anyone else on our block, but we all look out for each other and it's as close to family as I've seen without being blood relations (or maybe closer). Our neighbor Kathy M-G. has made it her business to know the birthday of ALL of us, celebrating each one with balloons tied to the rails of our stoops (yes, we actually have stoops here!), and she sometimes bakes each of us a cake, **_yum_**! We all sound the alarm to each other when the lunar tide from the bay is getting too high, threatening the parked cars on the street; this includes Rob and Trish M., Scottage Cheese and his wife Dashima C., Gil L., Maryanne N. and her wife Donna K., Grace A. and her husband, the author of the block's online blog (now defunct) version of Poor Richard's Almanac, Peter M. (Peter is also known as Walter Mitty). Frank E. and Debbie D., who live at the top of our block work with New York Families For Autistic Children, organizing events to raise money and awareness for those on the autistic spectrum. Every first Sunday in December is a motorcycle ride from Forest Park to our local American Legion to benefit the NYFAC' – God bless them, they're doing God's work for sure! Maryanne, Donna, Scottage Cheese (his name is actually Scott V.), Dashima, Grace and sometimes us are involved with the local Kiwanis chapter. Beyond our block is the local civic organization that looks out for the well-being of our little community and has been very successful in what it's accomplished. This all comes back to illustrating why and how this man attracts and is attracted to people with integrity – you can only give from whence you have…

In any event, please understand that this is merely the documented experience of someone who grew up in the mid-to-late 20th Century, in the 1950s and 60s, in one corner of Brooklyn. This, when Brooklyn was not a destination for anyone of means or with any pedigree: you were a success if you got out! If you walked down President Street or Carroll Street, between Third Avenue and Nevins Street, or on Third Avenue between President and Carroll at that time, you wouldn't see Michelin-rated restaurants, multimillion-dollar condos, high-end hotels, or luxury apartments because back then, there were multi-family tenements with open windows and curtains billowing out (Window guards?? What window guards!!!), kids playing street games, running in and out of the busy traffic-ridden road and back onto the bustling sidewalk, and cooling off in an open fire hydrant (a.k.a. johnny-pump), during the heat of the summer. It was the crossroads of Naples, Italy and rough and tumble South Brooklyn. Many of today's newer residents of this part of Brooklyn have referred to the people still there from earlier eras as "leftovers." But that elitist dismissal suggests a failure to realize that those "leftovers" were the pioneers of this former Italian-American ghetto, living there when it was a neighborhood to be avoided unless you knew someone. Again, this is describing a time that was long ago and far away, but for the memory of those who lived it.

The author, who is proud of his roots, has evolved. With all humility, he has said: "I won't ever forsake my neighborhood, but there is no denying that our pro-Italian mentality was limiting and not the reality of the world. In fact, you could say we were racist, no matter that most of us had no contempt for other traditions or ethnicities; we were just ignorant of our errant views." Although I can attest that my wonderful husband has evolved and solidly grown, we can't speak as definitively about the direction of the rest of society.

Times have changed and so has the author, although he is and has always been ... a stand-up guy.

-Sophia Vailakis-De Virgilio

THREE GENERATIONS OF FAMILY

THE AUTHOR AND THE WOMAN BEHIND HIM.

A Little Photo History of My Family and Me

ON THE LEFT, MATERNAL GRANDPARENTS WEDDING PICTURE. ON THE RIGHT, MY PATERNAL GRANDPARENTS, (THE TWO IN THE TOP ROW) AND THEIR CHILDREN: MY DAD IS SEATED ON THE FAR LEFT. THE REST ARE MY UNCLES AND ONE OF MY AUNTS. AND YES, TAPE IS HOLDING THIS SHOT TOGETHER.

BOTH SETS OF MY GRANDPARENTS HAD LITTLE FORMAL EDUCATION. THEY WERE PEASANTS WHO MIGRATED TO THE U.S. AT THE BEGINNING OF THE 20TH CENTURY. BUT JUST LOOK AT THE DIGNITY THEY HELD THEMSELVES WITH.

MY PARENTS WEDDING PICTURE. THE FLOWER GIRL WAS MY COUSIN MARYANN AND MY MOTHER'S GODDAUGHTER FOR BAPTISM AND CONFIRMATION. MY UNCLE FREDDIE WAS THE PILLOW BOY

DAD IN HIS MOTORCYCLE GARB AND MY MOM.

DAD ON HIS HARLEY, I'M PRETTY SURE IT WAS A 1954 PAN-HEAD.

THE FOLKS ON THE BEACH. NEITHER OF THEM KNEW HOW TO SWIM.

THESE ARE MY BRONZED BABY SHOES.
HOW MANY OF YOU STILL HAVE YOURS?

SOME PICTURES OF ME AS A BABY. MY WIFE SAYS I LOOKED LIKE AN ANGEL WHOSE CHEEKS YOU WANTED TO PINCH, THEN GREW INTO SOMEONE YOU WANTED TO SLAP!

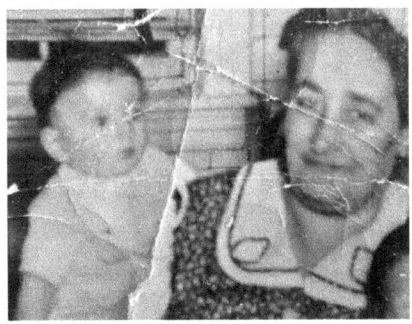

THIS WAS MY MATERNAL GRANDMOTHER HOLDING ME. AS YOU CAN SEE, THIS PICTURE HASN'T HELD UP AS WELL AS SOME OF THE OTHERS AFTER THE MORE THAN 70 YEARS.

FROM THE DAY I WAS BORN IN 1950 UNTIL THE DAY SHE DIED IN 2021, THIS WONDERFUL, BEAUTIFUL WOMAN, MY GODMOTHER, NEVER WAVERED IN HER LOVE FOR ME.

THE EARLY YEARS OF MY LIFE-LONG PARTNERSHIP WITH MY COUSIN EMILY, MY PARTNER IN CRIME! SHE WAS THE FLOWER GIRL, AND I WAS THE RING-BEARER/PILLOW-BOY. JUST LOOK AT THAT MISCHIEVOUS EXPRESSION ON HER SWEET, ANGELIC FACE. I WAS BEING GOOD THAT DAY! SHE AND I ARE SIX WEEKS APART AND FLIP SIDES OF THE SAME COIN.

WHEN I GRADUATED FROM KINDERGARTEN, WITH MY PATERNAL GRANDPARENTS
IN FRONT OF THEIR HOUSE.

MY YOUNGER BROTHER AND MY
SISTER, WHEN SHE WAS AN INFANT.
SOMEONE DREW ALL OVER
THIS PICTURE.

MY YOUNGER BROTHER.

MY BABY SISTER... AS A BABY.

MY WIFE SAYS
DENNIS THE MENACE AIN'T GOT NUTTIN ON ME.

10

US BROTHERS AGAIN, BEFORE OUR SISTER WAS BORN. MY DAUGHTER THINKS I LOOK LIKE A LITTLE ADULT MAN.

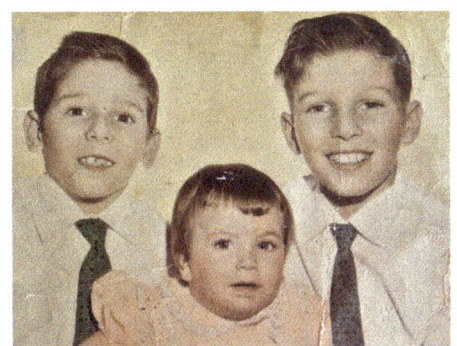

THE THREE OF US. MY BROTHER AND I WERE FILTHY, BEHIND THE EARS AND FROM THE WAIST DOWN. DOESN'T MY SISTER LOOK LIKE SHE'S BEING TERRORIZED??

MY BROTHER AND HIS GODFATHER, OUR UNCLE ANGELO. AS WAS TRADITION BACK THEN, MY BROTHER TOOK UNCLE ANGELO'S FIRST NAME FOR HIS MIDDLE NAME WHEN HE WAS CONFIRMED. IN OUR FAMILY, THERE WERE THREE MICHAEL ANGELO'S, TALK ABOUT BEING ITALIAN!

MY BEAUTIFUL SISTER WHEN SHE RECEIVED COMMUNION.

AN ANGELIC-LOOKING ME, BUT MY WIFE ALWAYS SAYS, "WHO KNOWS WHAT WAS GOING ON IN THAT HEAD!"

CATHOLIC GRAMMAR SCHOOL GRADUATION.
MY DAUGHTER SAYS THAT
I HAVE A ROMAN NOSE IN THIS PICTURE ...
ROMAN ALL OVER MY FACE!

HOW MANY OF YOU
REMEMBER THIS?

Um Frum Brooklyn

My life began in December of 1950 in South Brooklyn (but geographically is actually northern Brooklyn), as the eldest of three children to Joseph and Louise De Virgilio; we are Italian-American (100% Neapolitan, Italian). I have a sister Anna and a brother Michael, who I love very much. We lived in an apartment house on Third Aven between Carroll and President Streets, where two-thirds of the families in the building were my relatives, and the other third were also related but to each other and not us. That building was our Holy Grail because everything revolved around it and lots of funny things went on there too. As I was writing this book, I thought to myself, how grateful, honored and blessed I was and am for the time I've had on this earth, for being an Italian-American from Brooklyn, for our traditions and heritage, and to see the Brooklyn Dodgers win their only World Series in 1955. How many of us can say that? That same year, 1955, I started my formal education at a Catholic grammar school right around the corner from me. My high school career started at a trade school in Coney Island and I finished at a different high school in Park Slope, where I later worked as a teacher and met legends in the physical education field.

Speaking of influences in my life, get ready because I'm going to name names (which we *NEVER* did in my neighborhood), but I'm doing it now because they helped shape me into the person I am today. I got brought up by Italian-American parents and immigrant grandparents who came from Italy, all of whom I learned so much from without them saying a word to me. Not once in my life did any of them ever sit me down to tell me about the birds and the bees or anything else. Growing up, seeing how my parents and grandparents did everyday jobs was the language they used to tell me how to live my life, not words. Some of the most rewarding times for me was when I helped my father and his father (my paternal grandfather) with picking fruit and other produce at the market they went to, to buy and then load it all onto their truck for them to sell it later in the morning. Also, when my maternal grandfather got grapes to make homemade wine, I would help him carry cases of the grapes into the cellar where the wine vat with the crank to crush the grapes was (no, he didn't stomp the grapes with his feet like Lucille Ball did on "I Love Lucy"). I also helped my mother's father with shoveling coal into the coal furnace that heated our building when he was the superintendent. Later on when I blew my nose, it came out black!

This deserves its own paragraph because I gotta say as much as I loved helping shovel coal into the furnace, watching when the coal was delivered was fun because it was this whole process. The coal men drove up to the front of our building in a truck; one guy opened a trap door that was at the top of a chute on their truck for a bunch of coal to slide into these heave-duty 55-gallon wooden barrels, a lot like the ones used for whiskey (like the one below) ... which are heavy enough when nothing's in them.

HERE'S WHAT ONE OF THOSE GORGEOUS BARRELS LOOKED LIKE: THEY PROBABLY WEIGHED A GOOD 50 OR 60 POUNDS WHEN THEY'RE EMPTY.

When the barrel was full, this same guy would close the trap door, pushing against the momentum of a truckload of coal, then roll the full barrel along the sidewalk to the opening of the cellar of our building – it was basically a hole in the sidewalk with two metal doors that were almost perpendicular to the sidewalk when they were open, with a bar hooked into each door to keep them from slamming shut – they closed flat to the sidewalk (more on our building's cellar door in "Stories").

HERE IS WHAT THOSE BASEMENT DOORS LOOK LIKE CLOSED.

The cellar opening, with the building's coal chute (a two-foot wide slide with six-inch sides/walls), was what the first guy used to slide the barrels down, with a second guy waiting in the cellar at the bottom of that chute to catch each barrel. That heavy barrel, full of coal, being caught by another guy who watched it hurtling down that chute towards him, boggles my mind. The guy in the cellar then rolled this full barrel to a room specifically for the coal right next to the furnace and dumped it out into a pile on the floor. Each delivery was about 30 full barrels of coal, which took these guys about an hour and half to complete because they were built like brick-shithouses and they had this process down to a science.

Now, when it was time to feed the furnace, we shoveled from that pile of coal in that room into a wheelbarrow that we rolled it into the room with the furnace and shovel right from the wheelbarrow directly into the furnace opening – this was our process. We shoveled the coal to the back-left, back-middle and back-right. Then we shoveled to the middle-left, middle-middle, and middle-right. Finally, we shoveled to the front-left, front-middle and front-right. It was about a six-inch layer of coal that we shoveled in there twice a day, usually piled on top of coal that was already red hot because the furnace was constantly on during the winter, burning earlier shovels of coal heating the building, and we knew we were finished when all we saw was that six-inch layer of black coal in the furnace. During the summer, only the hot-water-heating-stove was on and the coal used for that was bigger, like small bricks. That stove was basically a pot-belly stove. Don't ask me how big the furnace to heat the building was because I was a kid and all I knew is that it was much bigger than me. My grandfather used the ash from the burned coal when it snowed to throw in front of the building for traction; we didn't use salt back then and we tried never to waste anything, including ash.

I was ready to say that most of the people who influenced me were men because of the times back then and the roles men and women were in. But that's not the whole story because my father was a blue-collar guy who worked a lot. He went with my grandfather really early in the mornings, like 1 a.m., to be able to get the best fruit to sell later in the day as fruit peddlers. (Any of the fruit that my grandfather and father didn't sell that morning came back home to us at the end of the day.) After that, my dad went to the piers as a longshoreman, so he wasn't home all that much. My mother and grandmother were homemakers (housewives was another old-time term for stay-at-home women), so when I came in from school, it was them, the women, I was around most of the time in my early years, making their impact foundational. But as I got older and as was usually the case, boys and girls separate as we go to the people we're supposed to be like and for me that was the men. That's when many of the men in my life became towering influences. But I can't forget the impact of the Irish nuns, Italian priests like Father Arthur L. and the towering lay educator, Enzo T. I met both of them at my Catholic grammar school when they opened our Recreation Center (the original letters on the sign mounted above the Recreation Center are still there and in good shape today). I can go on and on about Enzo because he was a second father to me, even though he broke my nose three times… tough love – I'll talk more about him and Father Arthur in later chapters. There was also a bunch of street kids in South Brooklyn (like I said, it's really northern Brooklyn) who were my friends, mostly Italian-Americans like me, and I was the youngest. We hung out in candy stores, empty lots, hallways, recreation centers (there was more than one) and any other place that could hold 10 to 15 guys, and together, we learned about life on the streets of Brooklyn. The Dead End Kids, Bowery Boys and The Little Rascals had nuthin on us.

Our neighborhood was alive; it was full of kids, adults, places of importance and all sorts of goings-on. These places we went to had their own personalities and influence. Like the Recreation Center, which was also known as the Youth Center, that was run by Mr. De Vito (until Enzo T. and Father Arthur took over in 1964 and added onto the long list of already existing programs), where on Wednesday nights, it was bingo night, also known as "oh shit night" because when the one person who hit (spelling out the word B-I-N-G-O) would yell out, "BINGO!," everyone else would say, "Oh shit!" Then on Friday nights, we had Boys and Girls Scouts, alter-boys and later on was a dance (confraternity). On other nights, there was roller skating, basketball and the all-important neighborhood 'battle of the bands.' And if we weren't playing basketball in the Youth Center, we'd open the side door and there'd be guys playing football or poison ball. When it was warm enough, we went out the back door to play Stickball (more on these in the "GAMES" chapter). Outside of the church on Christmas Eve, the Nativity statues finally saw the baby Jesus placed in the manger, and the big church, the little church **and** the Youth Center were all full with people because **_everyone_** came out and went to midnight mass... it was an occasion!

Around the corner was Loozeen, my friend's grandmother, who sold the best lemon-ices that had real bits of lemon in them. But the big treat was when she turned on the light that was above her door (waaaaayyyy before Krispy Kreme became all the rage turning on their light when they had fresh baked doughnuts), because that's when we knew she made galzones (a.k.a. calzones) – 10¢ for small ones with only mozzarella cheese, and 25¢ for large ones that had mozzarella, ricotta and ham, I'm salivating now thinking about it! The oil Loozeen used to fry had to have at least 10,000 miles on it... which is probably why those galzones tasted so good! Then there was Wagner's bakery where we got Wagner pies that were about 6" in diameter and cost maybe a nickel. And of course, being the little broke connivers that we were, we stuck our thumbs in those pies so we could get them for free or a discount – the people in that bakery must have felt bad for us because how many times can the same bunch of kids always just happen to find the damaged pies. John's candy store was where we got nickel pretzels, 1¢ candy, bottles of sodas sitting in ice water in the Coca-Cola bin.

THIS IS ONE OF THOSE COOLERS WE DUG THROUGH TO GET SODAS, BUT YOU'D BE UP TO YOUR SHOULDER WITH THIS ONE, THROUGH ALL SORTS OF ICE WATER, FOR THAT ONE BOTTLE YOU WANTED. BY THE TIME YOU PULL YOUR ARM OUT AFTER DIGGING FOR JUST 1 TO 2 MINUTES, YOUR HAND MIGHT BE SO NUMB YOU MIGHT NOT BE ABLE TO FEEL IT OR THE SODA YOU THOUGHT YOU GRABBED. HOW WE DIDN'T GET FROSTBITE AND LOSE FINGERS IS A MYSTERY.

You had to roll up your shirtsleeve and then plunge your arm, usually up to your elbow, into that icy water to feel around for the coldest soda bottle. And before our friends noticed what we were getting, we would yell as quick as we could, "Thumbs down!" to mean that we were not going to share the soda – because if someone yelled, "Thumbs up!" before that, you had to share your soda. There was also Smiley's hot dog stand, Mary's grocery store and Joe's grocery store making this triangle on Third Aven, and we went to each one for something different. Mary's made the best tuna fish sandwiches, Joe had great ham sandwiches with fresh ground 8 O'Clock coffee, and Margie's (we called her Mahgahlod) was one block over. We went to Margie's for meatball sandwiches, egg-creams and ice cream sundaes. She was also open late, so we went there to hang out at night. All of these great places for different foods or candy forced us to strategize our day because we might only have 15¢ or 25¢ for the day from our parents and had to choose what we got from the stores... or do we wait for the Mr. Softee ice cream truck to get a cone or a chocolate éclair when he came after dinner time? Then again, maybe we grubbed money from another kid, or one of our uncles, (my Uncle Angelo was always good for extra money), then we could have a feast!

Summers in South Brooklyn (don't forget, it's really northern Brooklyn) were the best, besides tar-beach (laying out on someone's roof to get a tan) and cooling off in a Johnny Pump, we couldn't wait for the block parties. Weddings were another great bash because they were not at all formal. We mostly saw "football weddings" which was when, after the couple finished getting hitched by the priest, the bride and groom would go to the table with a huge bunch of sandwiches of all types, tightly wrapped in wax paper, pick them up one-by-one, and toss them to each guest – and if anyone else wanted to help get the eating started for the hungry guests (and likely themselves), they just jump right in and tossed a few sandwiches to whoever. This is how we lived: walking around the neighborhood, looking for different games to play with different kids, go to whatever store to get the treat that each store was known for and take part in whatever party was going on at the time because if we weren't actually blood-relations, we were still family because we lived in the same neighborhood.

This was our corner of South Brooklyn (let me be sure to tell you that it's actually northern Brooklyn), where about 175 kids lived (I'm sure I'm forgetting some, so the number might be even higher), and none of them/ us were strangers. Then, there was probably another dozen kids who came in from other nearby areas to hang out with us. For example, my friend Bobby C. came from Butler Street. But the sub-section of South Brooklyn (if you need to find it on a map, you gotta look in northern Brooklyn) I'm talking about was starting from President and Nevins Street, up to Third Aven, left along Third Aven to Union, right up Union to Fifth Aven, right along Fifth Aven to Garfield, right down Garfield Place (by the way, 38 Garfield Place was where Al Capone once lived before he went to Chicago), to Fourth Aven, another right onto Fourth Aven, Fourth Aven to Carroll Street, left down Carroll, down Carroll

Street back to Nevins Street, right onto Nevins and along Nevins, back to Nevins and President, a six-block area. If you strung those blocks in a straight line, long-ways, they might be 6 tenths of a mile in length, so that's how dense the area was in population with kids back then, I don't know about now:

THIS IS A MAP OF THE AREA, WITH THE RED OUTLINE (NOT MEANT FOR RED-LINING IN MY CASE), OF WHERE ALL THE KIDS I HUNG OUT WITH LIVED.

In case you weren't sure, I'm very proud of my Italian-American heritage. These days people get ancestry tests to find out that they have other nationalities in them. I will state here and now, I am not any other nationality, I know I'm 100% Neapolitan or Napolitano (in non-Brooklyn-Italian-slang, Nah-poh-lee-tahn). Why do I know this? Because my parents and grandparents told me, and that's good enough for me. The way I got brought up, and in my eyes, any other self-respecting Brooklyn-Italian will not look at anything but what they saw, lived, and loved as they were growing up. If I make the cut to go to Heaven, (I know that's where my parents and grandparents are), I will meet St. Peter, God and my relatives would be next, waiting to hug and kiss me, pinch my cheeks, then kick the living shit out of me from one end of Heaven to the other because I took an ancestry test, meaning, I didn't believe them, especially my grandfathers! In particular, my maternal grandfather would say, in his gorgeous, unique brand of broken English, "What? You was not believe what you was be? I was tell you; you was born Italian, you lived Italian and you die Italian, but you was need a test?!" Anyone who grew up the way I did or with strong elders should understand what I'm saying. How many of you agree?

Now, I want to give everyone reading this fair warning: some situations I describe may be hard to read because back then those experiences with the adults in my life were... well... brutal. Let's be honest, today, those adults would be up on charges of child abuse and assault, *but who would report them in my neighborhood?* The difference is, this makes me who I am today, and my family was trying to do right by me because they loved me, which was the case for most of the adults back then who used physical discipline on kids. Both of my grandfathers didn't have too many tools, so they did what they knew, which was being physical. But despite that part of their personalities, they were loving, honorable men. Unfortunately, they often felt like they were up against it, so this was how they handled things, it was also the way the world treated them and all of us back in those days. I also realize that in my case, I really needed to be straightened out because I was headed for real trouble, ***not mischief***. So please don't think too badly about some of the adults I talk about and how they treated us back then. None of us in today's world can wrap our minds around what it was like to be them, to really understand the lives of my elders who were born at the beginning of the 20th and the very end of the 19th centuries: people like my grandparents who were, and came from peasants, and were fleeing the brutality of fascism in Italy that was taking hold, as well as extreme poverty and the random loss of property (they were usually robbed of what they had by someone else with more power). Life is hard today, but the level of inhumanity they faced every day at that time is nothing any of us today can know. At the beginning of the 20th Century, they had to fight for everything they had and were caste as an underclass. They were kept from a lot of legitimate work and had to fight hard to get any legal jobs to support themselves and their families. Italians back then were shoe-horned into Italian ghettos (the practice of red-lining, segregating neighborhoods by nationality, sticking unwelcome groups into undesirable locations) and they had no standing in society. They (we) were treated like shit and looked down on by non-Italians who called us 'dagos', W.O.P.s, 'Guineas,' 'zips,' 'greaseballs,' thought of as not being white, which all started to change from about the 1970s, 80s and 90s. Vince Lombardi is an example of how Italians were viewed back in the mid-20th Century; the New York Giants wouldn't hire him either because his skin was too dark or his name ended in a vowel; whatever the reason, it came down to him being Italian. Just remember, we should all be careful about judging other people unless we've walked a mile … or ten … in their shoes. It's important not to impose today's standards on a time that's long gone. It's hard for people today to understand how far we've come in this world in so many ways, that folks back then came from a completely different world and worked with a whole other set of rules and ways of doing things than we do now. But most important, those were my elders, my family, my roots and they probably saved my life.

INTRODUCTION

Good morning, good afternoon or anything good, when you decide to read this book. My name is Leonard Michael De Virgilio and let me start by saying how I always ask my close... and... not so close friends, "How many times have you been at some get-together telling stories and someone says, 'We have to write a book'?" Well, here's mine and it's VERY Brooklyn-centric. Now you may ask yourself, "Ok, another book about Brooklyn. What's so different about this one?" Well, to be quite honest with you, I don't know because number one, I am not a reader and two, I am writing this book from different people's points of view, all mine, but at different points in my life: Some parts written as a little kid, then as a pre-teen and into my early teens. I have to tell you, I decided to split this into the early years and a second book for my later years because this would have wound up being more than 300 pages!

Even though the stories are a mix, this is a feel-good book; it's meant to put a smile on your face. I'll warn you now, I might repeat myself... just a little. Whether it's while you're reading "LANGUAGE: BROOKLYN SAYINGS – NO, NOT 'YOUR MUTHA,'" "NICKNAMES," "TRADITIONS," "GAMES," or any other part of this book. Feel free to have a look at the "Language" *section if you're unfamiliar with some of the terms I use.* But to be honest, I'm betting you might say, "Holy shit! I haven't heard that saying in years!"

It's funny, I asked a couple of friends I worked with to read parts of the book (they chose the chapters), and when I saw them later in the day, they gave me the response I was looking for; they told me it was entertaining, it made them laugh and gave them a good feeling inside of them. I couldn't be more ecstatic, happy or proud! Thank you, Michael, June and Antnee.

This book is filled with *stories, nicknames, sayings, traditions*, and a number of other situations and topics. I'm mostly writing this book the way I talk. If you could hear me, I have *dis* lovely Brooklyn accent, unless my wife sees fit to correct me, AND SHE HAS. Okay, and I'm not *da* best grammarian (how's *dat*, Blair?), and I'm not a writer. But where I grew up in South Brooklyn (did I mention that it's really northern Brooklyn?), we didn't have time to make complete or correct sentences as long as we got our point across. We New Yorkers are always in a rush! We didn't care if our sentences had everything like a noun, pronoun, adjective, etc... We spoke from our hearts and with our own shorthand. Like I said before, we would say, "You know *'dat 'ding*" and we all understood one another. Or if you wanted to get someone's attention, you might yell out really loud, "A!" or "O!" and for some strange reason, the person you were yelling to, knew it was meant for them and turn around. I coach swimming and I do this with my swimmers too, and it still works! Go figure!!

Many of *yous mighta* caught a few instances of *'dis'* instead of *'this'* or *'dat'* instead of *'that'* or *'da'* instead of *'the,'* and if it hadn't been for my wife editing this book, including the spelling of those words (she said I'd lose people because no one would be able to follow what I was saying), the whole book mighta been written that way. We can't forget *'dese'* and *'doze'* (my cousin Jerry was great at *dat*!) instead of these and those. As you read *dis* book, there will be more mispronounced, misspelled, slang words and incorrectly placed words as well because this is how I talk. You'll also notice that the word 'avenue' is shortened 'aven' because that's the way we say it downtown – my wife cracks up when she hears me say that because she wants to know why I can't spit out just one more syllable. Remember, we didn't have time for complete sentences, or in some cases, cutting a word down was easier too, but people know what I'm sayin!

I went to college in Dodge City, Kansas and there were a bunch of us from Brooklyn there. After I finished school, I stayed and lived there for a total of seven years. My Kansas cousins love the way we Brooklynites *tawk*. The interesting thing about Kansas folk is that they were and still are the closest thing to Brooklyn people I ever met. I still to this day, keep in contact with them. I have a family there that took me in and adopted me as a son and brother, and I will be indebted to them for the rest of my life.

Many of us born in the 50s may have forgotten some of our traditions because of 1967 (the Summer of Love), except of course, some of my friends on Third Aven or Fifth Aven because they were a bit more strait-laced. These days we go back to smoking cigars, talking Italian, playing Bacci Ball. It's the Red Hook Lunch Crew, The South Brooklyn Breakfast Club, the annual Carroll Street

Stickball game (in August or September), where people who are now spread out all over the country come back to Carroll Street, between 6th and 7th Avens, to play a game of Stickball – the newer residents of this part of Brooklyn had no idea what Stickball was when we started showing up a few years ago to play it, and if you're wondering, see the "GAMES" chapter. We also meet at the VFW for an old-timers' game of softball on Labor Day weekend. Whatever get-togethers we have, it's all about connecting, camaraderie and stories that get told about everyone, including people who are not with us, good or bad, and personally I don't know any bad (I guess I'm like Will Rogers who said, "I never met a man that I didn't like."). This is something we had, and a lot of the time took for granted because we didn't know what an important part of our lives it was until we got older. Now there's the new tradition of reunions for the past few years in Carroll Park for people who hung out there. I took my wife to the 2023 Carroll Park Reunion, and it wasn't just our generation but many, so it's also a way to get to know new people and make new memories. While we were at the Carroll Park Reunion, a woman came up to my good friend Gene and me, and she confused us, asking if I was Gene and if Gene was me, which shows how close Gene and I were back in those days, and we're still in contact today. The importance of these get-togethers comes through in how my friend Anthony (Antnee) shows it by getting a block of tickets to see a baseball game played by the Brooklyn Cyclones (they're the NY Mets minor league team) every year and then he calls a bunch of us to go to this game, refusing to take money for the tickets. So we all chip in for lunch before the game to treat Antnee, which doesn't compare to all those tickets. Of course, once we get to the ballpark, no one lets Antnee pay for a beer there either. Anthony is a guy who enjoys his old neighborhood buddies and we enjoy him!

HERE WE WERE AT ONE OF OUR OUTINGS TO SEE THE BROOKLYN CYCLONES. WHAT A GREAT BUNCH OF GUYS! MY BUDDY BILLY, A 9/11 FDNY HERO, IS SEATED AT THE BOTTOM-RIGHT SIDE, BUT HE'S NO LONGER WITH US AND I MISS HIM EVERY DAY.

Thank God all that lockdown insanity is over, so that all of us who live close by one another, or even if you live in another place, let's stop making excuses and let's get together! I read so many things on Facebook where everyone writes about how important our upbringings were and still are. So let's stop the bullshit, get off our asses and start returning to our old stomping grounds. Let's have fun like we did when we were kids. I guarantee a get-together will be great for the body, mind and soul (like the name of Country Joe's first album, "Electric Music for the Mind and Body"). It will last a lifetime. It seems like when we do get together, it's at someone's wake. *Remember*, caskets have no pockets, so spend your money before it's too late on new memories with old *and* new friends, or old memories with old friends.

Finally, I need to let you know that I was a kid who got into quite a bit of mischief and I'm detailing a lot of it here, so sit back, enjoy the ride, ...and hold on tight!

P.S. I'm leaving 2 blank pages after each chapter so you can write down your own memories, thoughts, experiences or anything else you might think I left out because none of these chapters are exhaustive. And also, you gotta remember, even though I've been able to recall quite a bit, I have a good memory for forgetting things... and if it wasn't for flash-backs, I'd have no memory for anything at all.

ODE TO BROOKLYN

Let me tell you what Brooklyn means to me; it's a state of mind. It's magical. A unique way of life. A spirit. A talk. A walk. It's its own person. It's like no other place in the world. It's nothing short of legendary. For example, nicknames, neighborhoods, foods, our accent, all sorts of ethnicities and that good-as-gold regular, salt-of-the-earth guy in old-time war movies who is the spoken conscience, the hero. Like William Bendix and Lloyd Nolan (even though Lloyd Nolan was from San Francisco, he sounded like a New Yorker!). And what is the infamous, authentic Brooklyn accent, you ask? Watch a Bowery Boys movie and you'll hear it when Leo Gorcey speaks (he was Slip Mahoney). But to be honest, the Brooklyn accent permeated all of New York City, unless you had a really sharp ear that could tell a Queens accent from a Bronx accent from a Staten Island accent. We all kind of got lumped together and the whole lot of us were told we all sounded like we were from Brooklyn. If we really break it down, the differences in how a Queens accent sounds in comparison to a Bronx accent and then the famed Brooklyn accent, each can be traced directly to the immigrants who populated each area and the countries they came from. For us, it was mostly Italians from Naples (some from Sicily and other parts of Italy), and that we mostly learned from babies how to speak English from people who spoke to us in Neapolitan-Italian flavored broken English. My wife tells me all the time that I sound like someone whose sentence structure and word usage is not based on English but Italian transliterations. For example, "That thing..." (said, 'Dat ding...'). If you were Italian, you picked up on our idiosyncrasies (How's that Blair!).

I was talking to someone who moved out of New York State, and they said as soon as they opened their mouth, people said, "You're from Brooklyn." People try to sound like us and have our mannerisms and it irritates me when on TV or movies someone with a Boston accent gets cast as the poor man's attempt to sound like a New Yorker. As an Italian-American from Brooklyn (for the purposes of this book, I will from here on mostly refer to Italian-Americans as just Italians), we speak with our hands and our hands are always moving. One time when I was telling a story, someone grabbed my hands and held them still; immediately, I stopped talking; it was like putting a muzzle on my face. We have our own language. Like I said in the Introduction, we swap 'd' for 'th' and vice-versa. We pronounce words like 'dees' instead of 'these,' 'dem' instead of 'them' and 'doze' instead of 'those.' We connect separate words like Longiland, instead of Long Island. Then we drop letters from words like the 't' in Atlantic to make it 'Alanic' or 'Balic' instead of 'Baltic,' 'gingerail' instead of ginger ale and then there's 'yerass' instead of 'your ass.' And, of course, we add letters where they don't belong, like inserting a 'g' in the middle of sandwich to make it sangwich. We also drop 'r's from words or put them where they don't belong, like 'liberry' instead of library or 'soder' instead of soda. It's a real, live dialect that makes it really clear where we're from. You might even call it another form of 'Pigeon English' which might be a generous name for our version of English. Whatever. It's how we talk.

Brooklyn is a borough of sayings (see the chapter, "LANGUAGE: BROOKLYN SAYINGS – NO, NOT 'YOUR MUTHA'"). You might hear some of these things said elsewhere, but I heard them in Brooklyn. We have our own sayings, you know, different ways of saying the same thing like, 'What do you think I was made with a finger?' to say, "Do you think I'm stupid?" And then there's, "Common sense it's called! But to some people, common sense isn't so common." Another is "I've been around the block," and "I *mighta* been born yesterday, but I spent the night out on the town." or "I mighta been born at night, but it wasn't last night!" more ways to say that 'I'm not stupid.' *"Do you catch my drift?"* 'You know what I mean?' 'Do you understand?' Some people where I grew up may not've had formal educations; our education was in the street, that's where our schooling was when we were young and we took it into adult life. It's our foundation.

We also have many illustrious nicknames and everyone I put into the "NICKNAMES" chapter are REAL, and even if you're from New York, they may be hard to believe. There are some people in the "NICKNAMES" chapter that I can tell you all about, but others, only that I knew someone had this particular nickname, and that's it. You had to see my wife asking me, "What else about this one, or that one?" or "Did you know their real name?" or better yet, "Did you ever meet that person?" She was ready to slap me off the back of my head because there were a lot of "I don't know" answers to her questions, but that was our neighborhood, and if you wanted to stay healthy, you didn't push your luck!

Brooklyn is far-reaching; it has tentacles, and we Brooklynites all know it. To further drive this point, I'll quote something from Reddit where they mention a Columbia University historian who said 25% of the U.S. population can trace their ancestry to Brooklyn because up to three-fourths of those who immigrated to the U.S. before 1970 came through New York and at least half of that group remained in Brooklyn for some time after that, or permanently. Well, that's what Reddit had to say, **but I feel** that at least about one-third of America has a connection with Brooklyn, e.g., people that know people who currently plan to or used to live in Brooklyn, people who name their kids Brook Lynn is another example. I can't really prove any of it beyond pointing to anecdotal examples but think about it for a minute... No matter how much I love Brooklyn for all it's given me, my family and I moved to southwestern Queens, and my wife had our neighbor Gil going one day when she said to him, "You know this is East Brooklyn." He said back to her, "No it's not, this is Queens." He looked across the street to our neighbor Al (our dearly departed, deeply loved, tell-it-like-it-is, elderly neighbor, and father of our friend and current neighbor, Rob) and said, "Al, where do we live?" Al, annoyed, looked back at Gil and said, "We live on [this] street, you dope!" My wife continued and said, "And Long Island is FAAAARRRR, East Brooklyn!" Gil then realized that she was screwing with him and they all laughed. It's in our blood; it's who we are. You also have to understand that it's a borough with neighborhoods like South Brooklyn (I'm not sure I said that it's really northern Brooklyn), Red Hook, Bensonhurst and other geographical areas, each with a unique ethnic identity and personality. My sister-in-law just mentioned how, to this day, someone right off the boat from Greece could conduct business completely in Greek, in Bay Ridge (that's where my wife and her family came from), and she gave an example:

> A woman they knew who had been born in Bay Ridge but grew up in Greece from infancy returned with her husband and son and needed to find an apartment. So she stood on a corner of some Bay Ridge thorough-fare for about 10 minutes, smoking a cigarette, until she finally heard some people passing her speaking Greek. This newly returned U.S. citizen asked the passing Greeks, in Greek, where she might find an apartment to rent and they pointed her to a building right up the street from where they were standing, that she and her family were then able to move into!

Many of the ethnic enclaves that once defined Brooklyn and much of the rest of New York are being reshuffled, being replaced with newer immigrant groups, like Sunset Park which used to be Nordic, then Hispanic, but is now very Asian. And Red Hook has been gentrified to the point of being unrecognizable (more on that later).

New York was, and to a degree still is, notoriously segregated by ethnicity even with the reshuffling, and most of us were happy in our own neighborhood; those of us in South Brooklyn (oh yeah, it's really northern Brooklyn?) really didn't know any other ethnic groups too well. Sure, there were a couple of Irish, Puerto Rican and Black kids, as well as a smattering of other non-Italian kids there, and I'm sure other neighborhoods had similar scenarios. But I think we had more of an impact on the non-Italians than any of them had on us Italians. Hanging out in candy stores, playing every street game known and made up on the fly, cooling off in the water of open johnny pumps in the summer, and going to a pool room in the winter was what we did. We knew what time we needed to be home for dinner, weekends and weekdays; that's how predictable our lives were... mostly.

So, let me ask you; what comes to your mind when you hear the name, "Brooklyn?"

STORIES

All the stories you're about to read are true, except one… I'll let you figure out which one! Anyway, none of the names have been changed to protect the innocent because in my neighborhood, there were no innocents, there were no guilty, just us being us. We didn't really get into trouble; it was usually mischief (unless of course it was something serious…). Like they said in The Naked City, there are more than 8 million stories in The Naked City, this is one of them. Who remembers The Naked City? Well anyway, like I said, I've been mostly dictating this book to my wife (so she can make sure it's cohesive), and I started to wonder how good my memory was about certain things, so I called my friend _Scooter_. He and I started hashing through story after story and he said he couldn't believe how much I remembered. I'm about two years younger than _Scooter_ and the other guys I became friends with through _Scooter_, but I looked up to them and wanted so bad to be like them that it was like I was studying them. I guessed I studied hard because he and I were taking words out of each other's mouths and my wife was in stitches laughing while listening to the descriptions of people and the situations we all found ourselves in.

So, I'm going to start this "STORIES" chapter by describing situations I got into. I started walking at 9 months old, that's when the world opened up to me and when the lives of all the adults around me were thrown into complete chaos, especially my poor, beloved mother and her sisters who were also like mothers to me.

What's In A Name?

I'm sure I said it before, but I'm saying it again: I stayed in different parts of Brooklyn, like Park Slope, Red Hook and South Brooklyn – geographically, South Brooklyn is really Northern Brooklyn, but what the hell did we know… We heard it was South Brooklyn, and we didn't ask any questions; this was our mentality. "New ig a nird," which in Italian means (probably Brooklynese-Italian) "don't say anything!" When gentrification started to really kick in, because of the notorious reputations of South Brooklyn and Red Hook, real estate started calling South Brooklyn 'Carroll Gardens' or 'Lower Park Slope' or the even slicker catch-phrase, "The Lower Slope," so they could sell houses easier (they did the same thing in Manhattan when they changed Hell's Kitchen to ... Clinton! *Really*???). Red Hook and Park Slope were no different than South Brooklyn, and they were right next to us. We did the same things, had the same neighborhood/street set up of apartment buildings, private houses, schools, churches, stores and the rest. But to a lot of people, you may as well go to another country if you went out of your own neighborhood. Like my Uncle Bovie said when we moved from the Big Building to just _across the street_, "People are going to act like they need two [subway or bus] tokens to come visit you now." I guess it's just human nature.

Anyway, as was pretty common for us, I spent a lot of time in bars, mostly in Brooklyn: Red Hook, South Brooklyn, The Slope and some in Manhattan, working as a bouncer or bartender and just hanging out. To quote James Cumley from his book, "The Wrong Case," "I can't trust a man who doesn't drink because a man who doesn't drink doesn't trust himself." W.C. Fields also said, "Never trust a man who doesn't drink." **They were wrong**. I trust Mike B. and Teddy V. and that's enough for me. In any event, among the many places where things happened, including meeting my wife in the bar I used to own, life happened *everywhere.*

"Lee-oh-nard, Venecah"

When I was about two years old, I tried to throw myself out of the 5th-story window of the big building on Third Aven. It started with me throwing a glass out of the window – a glass made of glass, not plastic. Sitting in front of the building was my grandfather and my Uncle Nat, and after that glass crashed to the street, they looked up and all they saw was my head popping in and out of the window. My Uncle Nat stood underneath the window while my grandfather ran up the five flights of steps to get me. He entered our apartment and fortunately enough, kept his composure and spoke to me in Italian, "Leonard, venecah [vieni qui], come to Grandpa." I got off the windowsill and walked to him, as my Uncle Nat was still standing downstairs, frantically looking and waiting to catch me in case I fell. When I went into my grandfather's arms, he held me and hugged me tight, went into the kitchen and asked my mother, "Do you know where your son was be?" (My grandfather spoke his own brand of broken English that we'll get more into later.) My mother, who was ironing our clothes, said, "He was right here..." she thought I was still in the kitchen with her, but I crawled away without her knowing (all it took was a few moments). My grandfather punched her in the head for not paying attention, which was the way things were handled back then, especially by him.

Here's Your Hat, What's Your Hurry?

When my mother gave birth to my brother, I was two years old and still every bit the handful. Her sisters, my Aunt Anna, Aunt Josie and Aunt Terry, took me to the hospital, and my mother wanted to see me dressed nice, so my aunts dressed me up in a spiffy suit and coat, but no hat. In the 1950s, a man was not fully dressed or respectable without wearing a hat (more specifically, a fedora). On the way to the hospital, we were passing a hat store (haberdashery); I spotted a fedora hat in the store window and *I wanted it*! I had it in my head that since I was dressed to the nines, the hat would be the coup-de-gras.

I'm not saying I was spoiled, **buuut** I will say that I was gabadoss (Brooklynese-Italian slang for thick-headed or stubborn). I pulled all my aunts into the store with me and wouldn't leave until I got that fedora. These women were saints! I really gave them no choice, and since this was not what they were expecting, no one was carrying any real money, so they were forced to pool what they did have together to get me a hat, and Murphy's Law, they came up a little short. Especially because once I put that hat on my head, I dug in (my wife said it was a temper tantrum), that hat might as well have been bolted to my head; I wasn't going to leave that store without it. Fortunately enough, the owner of the store recognized my plight; in reality, he had pity for my aunts because they were under the gun time-wise to get me to the hospital on time, so he actually was a shrewd businessman seeing a sale now, and maybe future sales with the good-will he was buying by taking less than the ticket price, and gave me the hat for the money my aunts had. So now, I was walking down 7th Aven in Park Slope on the way to the hospital, as proud as punch (or as happy as a clam, as my wife says... can *someone please tell me* how anyone can tell when a clam is happy? I've never seen a clam smile, have you?? Where the frig does this phrase come from!?!). My aunts and my mother had coordinated a time for when she'd be by the window so she could see me on the street while she held the new baby for me to see because children weren't allowed to visit people in hospitals, especially small kids who were too germy and a health risk to hospital patients. As I was getting closer, my mother was telling her friends in the hospital that her son was coming to the hospital. As we got closer, she spotted her sisters and when she saw me, she said, "But I don't know who that small man is." My aunts told me where to look for my mom, and I was so excited! I started furiously waving to her and pointing to the hat. Later on, my mother asked her sisters, "Where did he get that hat?" My aunts explained what happened on this toddle with the toddler, and that they would have been late if they didn't buy it for me because I was fixated on it.

"Someone Should Feed This Kid!"

A big tradition back in the '50s and '60s was that our parents dressed the boys up in long brown robes with rope belts on St. Anthony's feast day in June and take us to church, usually it was our moms who took us. Then and now, the church sells bottles of St. Anthony's oil, St. Anthony's metals and bread, all blessed by the priest. When my son was little, I had him take part in this ritual as well. Anyway, at the end of the ceremony, all the boys went to the front of the church where the priest was waiting to bless each of us with holy water and the nuns had lilies to give all the boys (I've read that lilies are a symbol of purity and goodness, but it's hard to imagine those nuns or priests ever believed we embodied any of those qualities with how they used to slap us and tell us that we'd all die violent deaths with our heads in the gutter... more on this later). The parents of us young, pre-school boys coached us to all go up together, and the older boys went with their classes – once a boy was out of the third grade at the latest, this was off our radar.

When I was three years old, we walked back home after the St. Anthony church ceremony (we only lived about a block and a half from the church), and my grandfather was waiting for us in front of our apartment building when we got there. He was so excited because it was my first St. Anthony's service, so he wanted a picture of me holding the lily. The adults stopped paying attention to me (*not the smartest move...*), because they were trying to find a camera and by the time they had it and were ready to take the picture, I only had the stem of the lily in my hand because I ate the flower. My grandfather was confused and probably a little upset because he had a deep love and a reverence for animals and flowers, and knowing him, he must have thought that my eating that flower was disrespectful to it, that its beauty should be undisturbed until its petals fell off. So, extremely irritated that anyone would desecrate a flower like that, that his grandson of all people didn't instinctively know to abide by his adoration of flowers, he turned around and called to my grandmother and said, "Millie, venecah! Leonard, he was eat the lily! He was eat the lily! Something was be wrong with that kid!" As if she would be able to explain this to him! But if you know what the old Italian men were like, they were the head, and their wives had to answer for everything that happened – my wife can attest to that till today, so I guess the tradition continues! Well, that phrase did not stop with my grandfather; it has echoed time and again throughout my life. To this day, as a 73-year-old, when I see flowers, I have to stop myself from eating them. Ultimately, we got the picture… but no flower, and then we went into my grandparents' apartment in the back of the big building to eat the *food* feast my grandmother made for this monumental occasion. I have to be honest; she really didn't need much of an excuse to cook up a storm like that, just a little nudge to justify it.

"Flour Child"

At some point, my Uncle Shorty started calling me Lenny D O'Sturoonz and even today, my Aunt Terry *still* calls me that – sturoonz is an Italian-ish term that people say when referring to someone who is a pain in the ass. Uncle Shorty used to tell me that they found me "on top of an ash-barrel," because I was so bad that no one wanted to admit to being related to me and that I had been left there! Isn't that fucked up??!! In today's day and age, everyone would be up in arms about traumatizing me!!

Well, here's some more… *Tales of Lenny D O'Sturoonz*: My other grandfather (my dad's father) used to raise Boxers, which is how we got our dog, Teddy, who was a brown Boxer. Teddy and I loved each other, we were partners, we used to play together, and he let me do <u>ANYTHING</u> to him. We were all set to paint our apartment (*the adults were…*) after removing all sorts of wallpaper, and the cans of paint were placed in the rooms where my mother was starting. A couple of my aunts came up for coffee, so my mother took a break, but after maybe five minutes, they told my mother, "Lou, he's too quiet," My mother was so happy that I wasn't under foot that she brushed it off and continued the non-Lenny conversation. Not too long after that, and with more urgency, they said it again, "Lou, he's too quiet!" At that point, my mom had the uneasy epiphany that I **WAS** too quiet, so she went into the other room and there I was with what she thought was Palmolive liquid hand soap covering my hair (how many of you remember Palmolive hand soap??), but when she put her hand on my head, it stuck exactly where she put it, as if her hand was being suctioned against my head. That's when it struck her like a ton of bricks that it was actually the gray wall paint. I can remember bending over the open paint can, dunking my head into the paint up to my eyebrows... just don't ask me what provoked me to do it because *that*, I don't remember! My mother was floored because this situation never occurred to her, and as she was frozen in horror, a now greenish-gray Teddy came tearing through and skidding into the room, which is when my mother let out a blood-curdling scream, prompting my aunts to come running in, and my Uncle Johnny to come running up three floors to our fifth-floor apartment from his apartment on the second floor. Now you have to understand, this was 1953, there was no such thing as water-based paint. It was all oil-based and most still had lead in them. My head and Teddy's body were covered in this toxic oil and lead mess! Back then, the only way to get paint off was with turpentine – this is one of my excuses for being a little nutz, I tell people that my brain was pickled in turpentine when I was a toddler as they were trying to detoxify my head. So my Uncle Johnny said, "Let's blindfold him." And ever so gingerly, using a rag they kept dipping in the turpentine, they took the lead paint off Teddy and me, trying hard not to let Teddy lick it or to let anything get into my eyes.

Not too long after the episode of my self-inflicted superfund, hazardous waste garnished head, making it necessary for my uncle to clean me up – same fifth-floor apartment – my mother was coming home from food shopping with a friend of the family, Danny. You gotta remember, we were all like family in our neighborhood, but Danny was so close with us that he carried a picture of me in his wallet. My mom was holding the groceries and Danny was holding me, because he loved me. They got up to our apartment door and since Danny had a free-er hand, he opened the door... then frantically closed it and said to my mother, "Lou, I don't believe in ghosts, but you have one running around your apartment." Hearing that, I started squirming in Danny's arms. So as not to drop me, Danny puts me down and of course I went right for the apartment door, flung it open and ran inside to get a look at this "ghost," don't threaten me with a good time! For who knows how long, our dog Teddy had been rolling around on the floor in the bag of flour that he busted open all over the place. Before either Danny or my mom could stop me, I dove right into the flour with my Boxer partner, now both of us rolling around in it, worsening the mayhem. Teddy had also been eating the flour and it made him look like he was frothing at the mouth, what people called a "mad dog," so Danny was afraid to go near him. But before any of the mess could be cleaned up, my dad came home from work and when he walked in the door, my mother looked at him with her arms drooping down toward the floor, ready to cry and said, "Look what he did! Look what he did!" My mother was so upset, maybe even feeling defeated, that while she was off-loading this latest tale of Lenny-inflicted turmoil, her whole body was going limp to the point that all of a sudden, she peed herself while standing in the middle of the kitchen with the flour all over the floor (that had to be one hell of a mess to clean up!). From that day on, when my father came home from a long day of work, the first thing out of his mouth to my mother was, "What did he do today??"

"I Lowered Brother's Ears"

According to my wife, to say I was a handful as a kid, is the world's biggest understatement. In my defense, *I was unsupervised*, but then again, an octopus on roller-skates would have had trouble keeping up with me (one of many "Lennyisms"!! My mother used to say that I aggravated her so much while she was pregnant with my brother, that it made him come out of her belly already circumcised – also known as aposthia, (It's extremely rare; only one of dozens of sources say that 1 in 10,000 children are born this way). Here's another of my numerous antics my wife points to:

Back in the 1950s, even though we had a washing machine, everyone hung their clothes outside on a clothesline to dry because nobody had a clothes dryer, including us. On one particular day, after my mom did our laundry, she needed to hang the wet clothes on the clothesline to dry and since we lived on the fifth/top floor of our apartment building, the roof was where we hung our clothes so she was actually about to go onto the roof. At this point. I was about four years old and my brother wasn't even two yet. She knew she couldn't have me on any roof with her, or I might try to throw myself off, or worse yet, try to throw my little brother off (see, "Leonard, Venecah") so she figured it was probably safer all the way around to keep me occupied with a 'big boy' task in our apartment – people used to leave little kids alone and looking after each other, all the time back then. She said, "Lenny, you watch baby brother, mommy's going next door for a minute." She didn't know it, but I fancied myself a barber and when she left, I grabbed a hold of a pair of scissors (they were probably about 6 or 8 inches long, maybe half the length of my four-year-old arm...), because as the older, "helpful" child, she did ask me to watch my baby brother! Well, I decided he needed a haircut right then and there. After all, giving him a haircut had to be even more of a help. My mom couldn't have been gone for more than 5 minutes, but she said that when she came back, she found me with my brother's hair in one hand and that huge pair of scissors in my other hand, within inches of my poor, terrified brother's head, as he was twitching, blinking and cowering in his highchair trying to lean away from me. I told her, "I give brother haircut!" She never left me alone with him or by myself again after that.

How Will I Miss You, If You Don't Go Away?

When I was about 4 or 5 years old, we were playing hide-and-seek: it was my cousin Kelly, my cousin Phyllis (both of them were at least 10 years older than me), my cousin Emily (who is six weeks younger than me), my little brother and me. I decided to hide in a closet; I threw all sorts of clothes on top of me and stayed there for about two hours because I fell asleep – basically, if I'm not moving, I nod right off, even now. Kelly and Phyllis knew where I was (at least that's what they told me...), so after they said they checked on me and that I was asleep, they decided to take my brother and my cousin Emily to go get something to eat, leaving me in the closet because it was nap time for me around that time of day anyway. When they got back, they started to call me and when I came out of the closet I asked them, "Did I hide good?" They said, "Oh yeah. Next time we play this game, hide in the same place." Looking back, should I be insulted or scarred? My wife says it shows what a pain in the ass I was.

Great Balls Of Fire!

My grandfather (my mother's father) was the superintendent of the apartment building when we lived in the big building on 3rd Aven, the Holy Grail! We kids used to help him shovel coal into the coal furnace to feed the fire and heat the building. Whenever I helped with shoveling the coal and I blew my nose it came out all black. On one occasion, my brother and I filled the furnace with all the coal it could take and I got the stupendous idea that the furnace needed a bigger flame to heat the building better, so I threw a can of benzene into it. All of a sudden, the biggest ball of fire I ever saw spit out of the furnace, directly at me and my brother, and burned the shit out of us. His eyes were saved by his eyeglasses and mine were saved because I put my hands to my face just in time. If the furnace door had been closed after the benzene was tossed in there, the whole furnace would have blown up and I would have been the proud recipient of non-combat shrapnel... if we even survived.

Greenie Stickum Caps

My cousin Jerry S. was another older cousin and a big kid who loved guns. On one occasion when he was babysitting my brother and me, he turned the lights off in our house to watch the sparks when we shot off the 3 cap guns with a big load of Greenie Stickum Caps. We must have been shooting them off non-stop because, by the time my mother and father came home and opened the door of the infamous 5th-floor apartment, they thought there was a fire with all the smoke and the smell of the caps we shot off. (I'm pretty sure those caps were filled with gunpowder because they left a strong smell.) My mother yelled, "The house is on fire!" But Jerry popped up from the couch to tell her, "No, we were just shooting off cap guns." My wife says it's no wonder I was such a nightmare growing up; I was surrounded with people who were just as worse as me!

Ang's Play-By-Play

My Uncle Angelo, who was married to my mother's sister, Lilly, was a big Brooklyn Dodgers fan. It was the last and deciding game of the 1956 World Series, the Brooklyn Dodgers against the Yankees, the last "subway series" between those two teams. My uncle came home from work (he worked for Pfizer) and went right to the TV to watch the game. He was a man on a mission because apparently, he bet his entire bonus on the Dodgers winning this time since they had won the World Series the year before in 1955, when "those bums" became kings! But the baseball gods had apparently flown the coup for our beloved Brooklyn Dodgers. The problem was the Dodgers were getting beat badly; they were losing 9, nothing! My uncle was feeling the stress and hoping for a miracle, and in his head, the harder he concentrated on the game, the more likely it would turn around. It was the bottom of the 9th inning, and the Dodgers were up at bat; my Aunt Lilly was putting dinner on the table, and she said, "Ang, the food is on the table." He said, "Wait, Jim Gilliam is at bat [but he grounded out], the Dodgers are not done yet." Again, my Aunt Lilly said, "Ang, the food is on the table." My Uncle Angelo's response was, "Wait! Pee Wee Reese is up [he tried to bunt, had a foul pop-up that was caught], but the Dodgers aren't done yet!" My Aunt Lilly, for the third time said, "Ang, the food is on the table, it's gonna get cold." My Uncle Angelo again put her off, this time saying: "Hold on! Duke Snider got on base; he hit a single!" Hope was not yet lost! My Aunt Lilly once again, dutifully said, "Ang, the food is on the table, come eat." My Uncle Angelo, with his last gasp of hope, stood up from his chair and answered, "WAIT! The Dodgers aren't done yet, Jackie Robinson is up!" Needless to say, Jackie Robinson struck out in his last game of his baseball career [he retired at the end of the season]; the game ended in a shutout and that's when it happened! As Johnny Kucks threw his last pitch with Jackie Robinson swinging and missing it, my Uncle Angelo exploded: the food and the TV went out their 4th-floor window! Everyone must have been home either watching or listening to that game on the radio because no one got hit with the food or the TV, and anyway, my aunt's and uncle's apartment was over-looking the empty lot between two buildings on Third Aven, which is still the same configuration to this day.

To add insult to injury, our beloved Dodgers moved to Los Angeles in 1958 and it only took them one year to win a World Series, when it took them 65 years to win the only one in Brooklyn. Dodgers' fans were long-suffering and because of that painfully prolonged first and only World Series win, you either loved or hated the Dodgers. The not-so-joking joke for decades was, 'If you had a gun with two bullets in it, and you had a choice who you could shoot: Hitler, Stalin or Walter O'Malley [the owner of the Brooklyn Dodgers], what would you do?' The response was, 'Walter O'Malley, twice!' It didn't come to light until decades later that the one responsible for the Dodgers not staying in Brooklyn was really Robert Moses, the famed and reviled NYC urban planner whose highways cut right through neighborhoods and hardened segregation in NYC till today. O'Malley was pleading with the city to build them a better stadium and he even proposed for it to be where the Barclays Center is now, but Moses was so all-powerful that his was the last word, which was, "No."

"Yippee Ki-Yay!!"

A couple of years after the above episodes, I met a kid on the corner of President Street and Third Aven who introduced himself by saying, "My name is Gerard." I said, "My name is Lenny." Gerard looks back at me and shrieks, "You're the kid who swings the cats around by the tail!" I immediately said,

"Not me!" Coming from my neighborhood taught me THE most important skill: how to stay alive by admitting to N O T H I N G. My friend who was with me, asked me later when Gerard left, "Did you used to swing cats by their tails?" I said, "Yeah I did, but fuck Gerard!" My friend looked back at me and said, "Yeah, fuck Gerard!" I also had enough brains NEVER to do anything like that around my grandfather (my dad's father) or for him to ever catch wind of me doing anything like that because he loved animals more than he loved his family. To give you an example, he had a Dalmatian named Dukie who died after getting hit by a car. For days after that, my grandfather was inconsolable; no one could talk to him, not even my grandmother.

And let me clarify this: there were a few neighborhood cats that came to our building because my grandfather (my mom's father) fed them to keep the mice and rats away, and because he was also an animal guy. A bunch of us kids hung around the cellar, and the cats wandered in and out. What I did was take a hold of their tails and lift their hind legs about 3 inches off the floor, with their front paws still on the ground, having them walk around in a circle by holding their tails, as if their tails were lassos (like the cowboys I saw on TV), so I wasn't actually picking them up and swinging them in the air. But still, I'm not at all proud of having ever hurt an animal in any way, even though I was only a young boy... But did I mention that I was *unsupervised?*

Sympathy Pains... *In The Ass*

When we were kids, my brother and I used to help my maternal grandfather take care of our apartment house because he was the superintendent. We swept the floors and stairs, inside and the outside sidewalk, shovel coal into the coal-fired furnace to keep the building warm in the winter (see "Great Balls of Fire!" to see how wise *that was...*), and help him put the trash out at the curb the night before garbage pick-up by NYC Sanitation. The entry to the building's cellar was on the sidewalk in front on the street, and there were two steel doors with diamond grating that had to be pulled up by handles (those handles slid flat against the doors when they were closed) and people could step on them as they walked the sidewalk because the doors were flat to the ground.

To open the doors, you'd need to first pick up those handles to lift up each door, one at a time, one on the right side and the other on the left side of the opening to the basement stairs. Then you'd need to place a long cross-bar that had hooks on both sides of it that slid right into the holes in a piece of metal (an L-shaped bar welded along the length of each door) on the underside of the doors, to keep the bar in place and the doors from slamming shut on anyone.

One day when I was about 7 or 8 (my brother was either 5 or 6 years old at the time), my brother and I opened the cellar doors and we didn't put the crossbar in place to keep them open. We sat at the top of the cellar stairs, pushing against the metal doors to keep them open, looking down into the basement. The next thing I know, one of those two heavy steel doors fell on my brother's leg, and of course, he started crying. There wasn't any sympathy from my grandfather because we should have put the bar in place to keep them open, or not touched the doors at all. So they take my brother into my grandmother's apartment on the ground-floor (which my Aunt Josie lives in that very apartment till today), they put him on the bed in their apartment, and he's still crying. I said to myself, "I have an idea to make him stop crying." I went back outside and slammed one of the cellar doors on my leg. Next thing, we were both on my grandmother's bed, and to soothe Michael's misery, I said to him, "Look, the cellar door fell on my leg too." Boy, did it hurt like hell, but I figured, if my brother saw us in the same boat that he'd stop crying – and he did just that. My grandfather had no sympathy for me either, because I had no business being near that cellar door again, especially after Michael got hurt by it.

So Much For Brotherly Love

For those of you who remember, in the late 1940s and through the 1950s, Lionel Trains were the toys to have, and my father bought us a set when I was about 7 years old. No matter who I was playing with, whatever toys we played with, I always acted like everything was mine and it didn't matter if it wasn't. In this case, the Lionel Trains were no different. My father put this set together and the trains went around in a circle on the track. As I'm entranced watching the train going in a circle, my brother decided to pick up the locomotive, which was the heaviest train-car, probably made of cast iron, and it made the train stop. I grabbed the locomotive out of his hand and hit him in the head with it. It didn't affect him that much because he punched me in the face. Needless to say, that was the last time the Lionel Trains came out.

Ride... Or Get Slapped Trying!!

My father bought me my first bicycle when I was 7 or 8 years old. And so, between my cousin Smiley, my cousin Johnny and my Uncle Freddie, who were all only a few years older than me, they all thought I shouldn't have training wheels and took them off the bike before I had a chance to take my first ride. They brought me around the corner from the Big Building (a block where a whole lot of mischief happened), for like a fifteen-minute lesson of how to balance on a bicycle... *for the first time...* They put me on the bike, pushed me along the sidewalk and let go; my cousin Smiley chased me while hitting me off the head with a Gil Hodges first baseman glove, my Uncle Freddie was running along my left side, slapping me with his right hand, and my cousin Johnny was on my right side slapping me with his left hand (because he was a lefty). It took me about 30 seconds to learn how to ride my bike because it was either I fall, keep getting the living shit slapped out of me worse than what they were already doing, or pedal really fast away from them. My wife said this was the Goodfellas slapstick version of teaching a kid how to ride a bike. My son and I considered teaching my grandson how to ride a bike with the same technique, but we realized that it might not be a good idea to pass that tradition along.

I'm My Father's Son

Times have changed, a bunch! With this story, if you know, any get-together we had, the men sat on one side of the room and the women on the other side. So all of my cousins and uncles were drinking at whatever party this was, and I went over to the men's table and asked to have a drink. One of my uncles piped up to ask 'why?' I promptly answered, "My father's not here, so I'm taking his place." With that logic, how could anyone say no? They proceeded to get me (*at 7 years old*) drunk. In today's day and age, this would likely be considered child abuse or corrupting the morals of a child, but I felt like a man, and that's how I was treated. Like I said, DON'T JUDGE!

Nadaward!

Then there was my friend Rachel, and her father was Danny, the same Danny who was there when the dog rolled in the flour. Rachel and I became very good friends as we got older, but she once told me that when she saw me and my mother walking down the block to her house because our mothers were friends and they would have coffee while we played, she worried about what I might do. And what did I do you might ask?? When I was about 7 or 8 years old, we were at her house and I was looking at all of the gorgeous fish in her fish tank, and they were looking back at me, opening and closing their mouths, which got me concerned for them that they were hungry (someone needed to feed these poor little guys!). So, when everyone in her house wasn't looking, I threw all the fish food into the fish tank, and the fish ate until they popped! (I doubt my mother told my grandfathers about this episode either, because I'm still alive...) She used to say to her mother, "There's the kid who blew up my fish! Ma! Don't let him come into our house! Every time he comes in, something bad happens."

No Way Out!

My grandfather (my mom's father) used to babysit us kids and watch TV at the same time, but you couldn't interrupt him when his cowboys were on, which seemed to be the only kinds of programs he watched. When I was about 7 or 8 years old, Grandpa was watching my cousin Emily, my brother, me ... and

Royal Rogers on TV when the phone rang and I answered it. On the other end of the line was my Uncle Tony who was a practical joker. He was trying to disguise his voice, but I knew it was him when he asked, "Is Mike B. there? Tell him there's a fire on the fire escape." My heart went into my throat and I said to my Uncle Tony, "Unc, not now, he's watching his cowboys." Uncle Tony insisted and again said, "Tell him there's a fire on the fire escape." I pleaded, "Uncle Tony, please don't make me say that to him." My grandfather heard me on the phone, he came over and with his unique broken-English he asked me, "Who was that be?" All I told him was, "Uncle Tony's on the phone," but I didn't want to tell Grandpa the rest of what Uncle Tony wanted me to say. My grandfather knew there was more to the story, and it was getting him more annoyed because I didn't tell him everything right away, and you didn't want to get Grandpa mad, *at all*. He then demanded I tell him what my Uncle Tony was saying, and at the same time, Uncle Tony continued to insist that I say it. I was in a no-win situation, a young boy in the middle of these two adult men – my Uncle insisting I tell my grandfather something he thought was funny, but I knew was going to get Grandpa really mad, and my grandfather whose blood was starting to boil because he always had to know what was going on. I finally decided I better just get this over with, so I blurted out, "Uncle Tony says there's a fire on the fire escape." My grandfather then immediately jumped into action; he ran to the sink to fill up a big pot with water and I ran right behind him, pleading, "Gramps, it's Uncle Tony, he's just fooling around, there's no fire." My grandfather tuned me right out because all he heard was that there was a fire... He took the pot of water to the window and opened the blinds as I continued to plead with him that, "There's no fire!" To no one's surprise, he looked out the window and saw... **no fire**. Grandpa then turned around, looked at me and said, "You was make a fool outta me!" He hit me, kind of a push-punch combo in the chest, and I went flying onto the couch from across the apartment. Before I could catch my breath to get off the couch and out of the line of fire, he ran over, grabbed my foot and started to bite it with his alligator death-grip, as I was squirming and yelling. He only stopped when my cousin Emily cried and of course, not a word was spoken about it afterwards. Let me tell you, I've been kicked by a mule in Kansas, I got hit by the horn of a bull in Pamplona, Spain, and I'd been hit by my grandfather in Brooklyn: I'd rather be kicked by the mule and gored by the bull's horn at the same time than get hit in any way by my grandfather. As my Aunt Josey always says, my grandfather was a truckman in the Fort Greene Meat Market and there were plenty of broken noses in there. If you didn't figure it out already, my grandfather had no sense of humor. How many of you had some adult in your life who threw beatins on you like that? My grandfather would be arrested in today's world, that is if anyone was stupid enough to turn him in. Again, in my neighborhood, you kept your mouth shut.

Mouth Control

Telling you that I was a pain in the ass, is probably unnecessary by now. Anyway, yes, I went to school with some lunatics, but when I was in the 6th grade, one day when there was all sorts of talking going on in class while the nun was writing on the board with her back turned, she yells, "Lenny, shut up!" My friend Al F. piped up and said, "Sister, Lenny isn't in school today." Later that day, I got a phone call from Al, telling me what happened. I think that's when I finally became aware that *I __was__* a pain in the ass; pa-so-y or wass-stay-gots, or sturoonz. Not that this realization changed anything for me because till this day, at 73, people either want to hug me or slap me... and my wife attests to it. Correct, Mrs. D.?

Margie

When I was a kid (about 8 years old), this woman Margie that we knew, didn't leave her house because she was so big, about 5' 2" and 300 lbs. All we ever saw of her was her head and an arm. Today, we'd call her a shut-in. Margie used to lower a burlap bag down from her window with a rope, onto the sidewalk, with money and a list of things she needed from the store. We kids used to go shopping for her, then put all of the groceries back into the burlap bag for it to be hoisted back up to her window and she'd usually have us keep a dime or a nickel as a tip. One day my mother wasn't feeling well because she had a real bad headache that made her need to lie down on the couch. Mom told me that since my dad gave her some cross necklace, she had constant headaches and asked me to take it to Margie because Margie was known to remove the evil eye from people by doing something known as "passing over the head." When I got to the front of Margie's building, under her window, I called up to her and she told me to come up. When I knocked on her apartment door, she told me to come right in (in those days, no one locked their doors), so I went in and I finally got a look at Margie in her entirety. Before I could say a word, she said, "Come sit down, I know why you're here." I don't know what scared me more, seeing Margie for the first time and how big she was, or the fact that she knew why I was there before I could tell her anything. She took the cross from me and held it as I watched her rock back and forth, sweating, moaning and mumbling with her eyes closed. She did all of this as if she was performing an exorcism for what seemed like forever but was only about 2 minutes. All of a sudden, she went limp for about 10 seconds, as if she got hit on the head, and I thought, "Holy shit! She's dead!" Next thing I know, Margie opened her eyes, handed me back the cross and told me, "Go home, your mother is alright." I was numb and couldn't move for about 10 seconds, then I grabbed the cross, ran out of her apartment, down the hall and I jumped down the steps in like one leap; I don't even think my feet hit the floor or the stairs. And let me tell you, if there was an Olympic medal for stair-jumping, I would have gotten gold! I ran from Margie's building on Presidents Street, made the turn onto Third Aven, ran up one flight of stairs to find my mother up off the couch, washing the dishes. When I gave her back the cross, she said, "I'm okay now." From the time I left with the cross, went and then came back home from Margie's, something other-worldly seemed to happen to my mother. Till this day, it still gives me creeps.

Just Say CHEESE! Ya Filthy Animals!!

When I was about ten and my brother was 8, we went to Prospect Park along with about a half-dozen other kids and we were all jumping this one mud puddle. When my brother jumped, he didn't clear the jump all the way, so that when he landed, one foot made it onto dry ground and the other wound up in the mud (my brother wasn't very good at jumping mud puddles, see the "Freedomland Ain't Free" story). When Michael tried to pull his foot out of the mud, his shoe got sucked in, never to be seen again. It was as if a bunch of hands were pulling that shoe off his foot, into the mud abyss, and none of the rest of us were going to route around in that mud to fish for that shoe! We figured it would suck us up too – back then, there were all these movies and tv shows where people were getting pulled into quick-sand, or eaten by "The Blob" (that was an early horror movie), gasping their last breaths, clawing their fingers bloody to keep from being sucked in, pleading with anyone to help, but of course, dying, so there was the boogie-man element to the power of that mud puddle! Well, that was the end of our mud puddle jumping that day. And being the big brother, I had to carry Michael on my back all the way to our house, which was about a mile away from the entrance of the park, because he only had one shoe. As we got closer to our apartment building, we saw all the adults on the corner of 3rd Aven, looking for us because we were supposed to take a family picture that day – but none of us kids remembered, and there were no cell phones back then for anyone to call us to remind us! My grandfather was so proud to see me taking care of my younger brother, but the closer we got, he saw how filthy we were and there was no time to bathe us because we were so late. The photographer made my parents just wash our faces and put clean shirts on us. We were so dirty that they didn't even have time to wash all that crust from behind our ears. We were photographed from the waist, up and head-on because if my brother or I turned our heads, you would've seen the layers of filth behind our ears. Even though she wasn't with us for our mud puddle jumps, she heard all the adults fussing about her grimy brothers that probably scared her and you can see the terrified expression on my baby sister's face in the final picture in the "FORWARD."

"Ah Come On Len, No One Knew What Was Going To Happen When You Guys Got Together!"

There were times when my mischievousness knew no bounds. My cousin Emily and I got into lots of mischief together. When I was about 11 or 12 years old, she and I made believe we were eating a chocolate bar and when my brother asked what we were eating, we told him, 'A Hershey bar.' Being we were all chocoholics, Michael naturally wanted some, so we gave him the whole bar, but it was actually Ex-Lax... and he ate the whole thing! We laughed so hard about Michael getting the Hershey squirts ... we didn't see him for two days after that.

Sing! Rocko, Sing!!

When I was about 12 years old, our friend Rocko moved to our neighborhood from Italy and was at our Catholic grammar school, at our talent show when we heard him sing "Santa Lucia." We were very impressed because of how much Italian he knew, but then again, *he was off the boat* (actually, probably a plane!). At some point, he tells us that he was going to sing "Blue Moon" in Italian and we all got excited that we were going to get our own private show of Rocko singing "Blue Moon!" He asked, "Are you a-ready?" then he starts singing, "Blue Moon-a-da. You saw me standing alone-a-da! Without a dream in my heart-a-da!..." So one of my friends said to him, "We thought you were going to sing "Blue Moon" in Italian?" Rocko said, "I did; that's how

I learned it." I guess he took a page out of Dion and the Belmonts' song, "The Wanderer," where Dion sings, "Oh well, there's Flo on my left-a and Mary on my right-a, and Janie is the girl well, that I'll be with tonight-a..." He also sang the song by The Diamonds, "Little Darlin" – "My dear-a, I was wrong-a..." Years later, I met Rocko at his mother-in-law's wake, and he said the person who talked him... (actually broke his balls) ...into singing was _Scooter_. The way Rocko put it, "_Scooter_ was a skutch!" Rocko said because he didn't think Rocko would sing like that, just adding an 'a' at the end of words in the song, and breaking balls back, that he was singing in Italian.

No, Your Other Left!

If anyone reading this has been to a block party in NY, maybe for you, but definitely for us, it was the first time that we could drink in front of our family. When I was about 12 or 13 years old, all of my friends and I got together and pooled our money, about $5 a piece, and got our own "table" at our block party on Presidents Street between 3rd Aven and Nevins St. Having your own table was a big deal because it made us feel like "the guys." We had franks, burgers, steaks, and a whole lot of beer. So, for us, it was more drinking than eating and believe me, we drank a lot. By the end of the night, which was at about 12 midnight or 1 am, I staggered home. When I woke up the next morning, I saw bedsheets all over the floor at the foot of my parents' bed, and my mother told me, "If your father hits you, I can't help you." So, I asked her, "Why?" Now, again, you have to remember that we were doing more drinking than eating and for some reason, I remember drinking two quarts of Rheingold Beer that my adolescent bladder wasn't used to. In the middle of the night, instead of making a left to the bathroom, I made a right... and where was that? Right into my parents' bedroom. But to me in my drunken stupor, I was in the bathroom, and the unfortunate location of the toilet was my dad's side of the bed! AND I LET LOOSE! To top all of that off, when my dad turned on the light, I had just finished. They said I had a big smile on my face and I staggered back to bed with that same shit-eating grin. My father told my mother, "Let me hit him now, because in the state he's in, he won't know _what_ hit him!" My mother said, "No! Because you might give him brain damage!" – _which people thought I had anyway_... When he came home later that day after my wrong turn, he told me, "Don't ever let that happen again." I dodged a major bullet with him; he had every right to throw a beatin on me!

It's A Wonder I Became A Teacher

In the 8th grade at my Catholic grammar school, Sister Mary Malachy asked everyone in the class, to raise our hands if we did the homework, so we all did. Well, Sister Mary Malachy that day selected _Pregnant Head_ to answer questions from the homework and when he said that he couldn't, she challenged him by asking, "I thought you said you did your homework?" He said, "I did, but a dog ate it." [And of course, no one ever used that excuse before!] So she told him to go across the street to his house (when we looked out the window from our classroom, we looked right at _Pregnant Head's_ house) to see if he could find any part of what the dog left behind, and during the five minutes that he was gone, she said, "I know that little boy is lying." When he came back, we were all trying to warn him that she was wise to him. Nonetheless, he told her that he couldn't find the homework, so she asked him over and over to confirm that he did his homework, and over and over he said, "Yes." She instructed him then to go to the blackboard and write the word 'abolish' because it was one of our homework words, but he completely misspelled it. And as expected, Sister Mary Malachy hit _Pregnant Head_, but not just a simple slap; she got creative this time. She slapped the back of his head into the blackboard and when it bounced back onto her hand, she kept slapping it back to the blackboard, basically dribbling it two or three times. Who knows why she finally stopped, she seemed to enjoy this sort of shit. The rest of us went on with our day because, well, it was Tuesday... This was nothing new. My wife said that with a name like Malachy, how could that nun not be full of malice. I spoke with my friend Al, who verified this story just the way I laid it out.

The abuse, torture and beatins were not just from the nuns, the priests got their shots in too, but in all honesty, we probably deserved 90% of it. Anyway, Father Ferdinand came to each of our classrooms to give out report cards, barking out his verdict of our marks. He would look at our grades, call our names out, and if he thought our marks weren't above 'satisfactory,' he'd announce what our marks were along with his insults that might go something like this, "What are you stoooooooopid?!" (right Jackie?). These priests and nuns were short on compassion and _l o n g_ on discipline. In spite of all the insanity, what I wouldn't give to go back to grammar school today!

Don't Walk, *RUN!*

Me and my friends were some bunch of blossoming young hoodlums, but in 1964, we finally met bigger bullies than us when Father Arthur and Enzo T. came to our Catholic grammar school. Father Arthur (we knew him as the hoodlum priest) was a very stern disciplinarian who took over the running of our school, and Enzo T. was the director of the after-school center; they both came from a parish in Little Italy in Manhattan and they already knew each other. The after-school center was open Monday, Tuesday, Thursday and Friday afternoons for things like football, softball and basketball. Wednesdays was reserved for ladies' bingo – how many of you remember that? This meant that aside from weekends, we had to entertain ourselves on Wednesdays too – so we played Stickball, off-the-point – also known as stoopball, poison ball – another name for dodgeball, but we played it with a spalldeen (a pink, Spalding sponge ball we all called a spalldeen) that we threw straight up in the air and whoever caught it after it bounced had control of the game (see the "GAMES" chapter for more on what games we played). But when that ball came down, like in rugby, it turned into nothing short of a scrum for us kids who were fighting each other trying to get the ball. It was a two-sided game, the older guys against the younger guys – I swear there had to be at least 50 kids in that schoolyard. So, if a kid threw the ball and after it bounced, you caught it, the kid who threw it was out. If a kid threw the ball and you missed it after it bounced, you were out, or if you got hit with it, you were out. To win the game, you had to get everyone on the other team out. We played these games year-round. It didn't matter if you got hit with that small ball on a warm day in the summer, or when it was cold in the winter; it stung just as bad. We used to get so caught up in these games and I was no exception. One afternoon when I had a lunch break from working at the grocery store, I decided to go join in a poison-ball game, and the next thing I know, my father comes down the street to tell me I was an hour late in getting back to work.

When I was in the 8th grade, my friend Opie and I were on the basketball team at school and our coach Father Arthur, to make us jump higher during practices, he'd stand on a chair, yell at us to jump as he grabbed a hand full of the hair on our heads in his hand and pull us up. We got fed up with the torture that Father Arthur was passing off as practice, so on a day when we had a basketball game, we told Father Arthur we didn't want to play anymore.

He told us to go down to the locker-room, get our stuff and go to the game. As we were going down to get our stuff, Opie and I were grumbling to each other about not wanting to play. We were sick of Father Arthur, and we both decided, "NO! We're not going to play!!" so we ran out of the door of the gym onto Denton Place, made a left up First Street, crossed Fourth Aven, and I asked Opie, "where are we gonna go?" He said, "My house," which was 1st Street between Fourth and Fifth Avens. The next thing, Opie yells, "Run Lenny, he's chasing us!" I turned and saw Father Arthur running up the street, holding up his robe in his hands with his bare, hairy legs, black socks and shoes, and those knees bobbing up and down like pistons of a car, coming after us fast! (Thinking about it now, seeing Father Arthur's legs like that felt like we were getting a gander at something forbidden, like getting an eyeful of someone's bloomers.) We ran up the stairs of the stoop into Opie's house where his family were all gathered, crying. I asked Opie what was going on. Opie said, "Don't worry about it, it's only my grandmother that died." All the stoops on the block looked the same, so Father Arthur had to ask some kid who was across the street, playing outside, where we went, and the little rat pointed out Opie's house. We were still trying to catch our breath when none other than Father Arthur knocked at the door. He comes in and before he could say anything, Opie's family thought he was there to express his condolences, but unfortunately, Father Arthur's mother had just passed away as well and so he was embarrassed for intruding, and probably still feeling the sting of his own familial loss. Opie was off the hook, but Father Arthur looked and me and said, "Let's go." He was furious at the whole situation, especially about going into the house of a grieving family. Now, Opie had one of those really high brownstone stoops… the next thing I knew, I found myself at the foot of the stoop because Father Arthur kicked me down the stairs the way he did that time in the gym (you'll read it below), I guess I have a face for being kicked down steps. As I stated, or as you may know, I later did stunt work in the movies and this was a great stair fall! I made plenty of mistakes in my life and one of the biggest was turning my back on Father Arthur, but bigger yet was when I hit the bottom of those stairs, I looked up at him and was about to run, but he said, "Don't run." Like a mamaluke, I stayed on the ground and the next thing, Father Arthur grabbed me with one hand on my shoulder to hold onto me and the other slapping me from Opie's house back to the Recreation Center where he told me to get my stuff and go home.

Opie's stoop   our school's recreation center

Like a good Italian Catholic boy, when I got home, I said nothing to anyone in my family and I went to school the following Monday. But when I got there, my teacher, Sister Mary Richard, told me to go home because since I was older than Opie, I got the blame and was being expelled from school. When I showed back up at home, my mother asked me why I wasn't in school, so I explained that I got expelled and she started to cry because everyone else's kids in the neighborhood either went to the same Catholic grammar school as me or another one a little farther away. And if she had to put me into public school, the nearest was P.S. 32 on Union Street, all the way on the other side of the canal, which was much farther from our house. We kept this whole thing from my father for a few days, and my mother went by herself to speak with Father Arthur who wanted no part of what she had to say because of how we embarrassed him. My Uncle Angelo took it upon himself to speak with Father Arthur who wanted nothing to do with him either, until my uncle said, "Can we speak straight?" Father Arthur agreed. My Uncle said, "Stop the shit, you weren't exactly an angel yourself. I know all about your life story, and you snuck a dog you weren't supposed to have into the seminary, so come on! Boys will be boys." It just so happened that there was a play being put on, all about how Father Arthur snuck this dog into the seminary while he was studying to become a priest, so he was caught dead to rights by my Uncle Angelo, but from what I understand, they let me stew for a couple of days before letting me come back to school. Thank you, Uncle Angelo, and thank you Father Arthur.

What Good Cat-Lick Boys

One occasion in the eighth grade, when my friend _Egghead_ went to confession, he stood out more than any others. As good Catholics, we always started by saying, "Bless me Father for I have sinned. It's been a week since my last confession..." as Catholic school students, we went to confession weekly... _Egghead_ told the priest whatever it was that he did. The priest _Egghead_ confessed to was Father Ferdinand who was short, with a shorter temper, who had a drawn out or even sing-songy way of speaking and a pretty thick Italian accent on top of that, who told _Egghead_ to do his penance which was probably a few Our Fathers, some Hail Marys and a couple Glory Bes To The Father. When _Egghead_ finished, he walked out of the confessional and immediately started cutting up with .... _Pregnant Head_! Sister Mary Malachy started yelling at _Egghead_ because she said she was watching him since he got out of the confessional, that he was sinning again, making a mockery of the church and that he should get right back in line to give confession again for having sinned so soon after his initial sacred confession of that day. _Egghead_ asked sister Mary Malachy if she was sure he needed to go right back into confession because he knew Father Ferdinand would blow a major gasket once he saw _Egghead_ back there so soon, but the sister insisted, so _Egghead_ dutifully returned for round two. When he got back into the confessional, _Egghead_ began by saying, "Bless me Father for I have sinned. It's been five minutes since my last confession..." and before he could get another word out, Father Ferdinand cut him off, yelling, "You were just heeeerrrre, get oouuut!" _Egghead_ said, "Calm down!" giving Father Ferdinand a bonus, a reason for more yelling, this time, "What do you meeeaaan, calm doooowwwwn! You're making a mockery of this sacrament!!" _Egghead_ then said, "Let me explain. Sister Mary Malachy saw me and Burt kidding around and told me to 'Come right back in here.'" Father Ferdinand said, "She whaaaat??" next thing, he stormed out of the confessional to go yell at Sister Mary Malachy which gave _Egghead_ a good laugh. But once _Egghead_ walked passed Sister Mary Malachy in the hall, she gave him a good slap on the head. By the way, if you didn't catch that, Al F. was known as _Egghead_ and Burt G. was known as _Pregnant Head_ – two great heads and two great friends.

There's another incident where a kid went to confession that went kind of like this: "Forgive me Father for I have sinned; it's been a week since my last confession. I sinned by doing the following things: [lied, stole, cursed... whatever else this kid told the priest], And Father, worst of all, I ate Chef

Boyardee ravioli out of a can!" Now, you have to understand the pride Italians have where it comes to food and how it was drilled into us, especially where it came to Italian food, that we should only eat homemade Italian food at home, and *NEVER FROM A CAN*! Food-pride case in point. I took my mother to a show at Lincoln Center in Manhattan and afterwards we went to an Italian restaurant to eat. My mother ordered lasagna, but she kept looking up at me as if for guidance, with this look of terror on her face as she was giving the waiter her order. So I went over to ask her privately what was wrong and she quietly told me, "I only ever ate Italian food in Brooklyn." For her, this restaurant being in Manhattan, was as good as eating a TV dinner or rotted food. I looked at her and said, "Don't worry Lou[ise], there are places outside of Brooklyn that can make good Italian food." So from the time she ordered to when the food came, she still had that worried look. When she finally got her entrée, she starred at it for what seemed like an eternity; she cut a small piece of the lasagna, braced herself with a long, deep breath, then slowly put what was on her fork in her mouth and after a few chews, with a look of total surprise, she made a twist motion against her right cheek with her right thumb and index finger (an Italian gesture to show that something is tasty), nodding with a great big smile! I looked at her and smiled back. I know she ate out at restaurants, but she was very Brooklyn-centric so everything for her happened in Brooklyn, including dining out.

I'm Not As Dumb As I Look!

One day, Father Arthur was sitting at the top of the bleachers in the gym of my Catholic grammar school and for some reason beyond anyone's understanding especially mine, I told him that when I get big, I was going to beat him up. As if he was expecting this, he didn't miss a beat and he said back to me, "Don't wait till you get big, if you have to do something, do it now." With that, I lost my mind, ran up the bleachers and when I got to where he was, he kicked me in my stomach, sending me down the bleachers, landing on my ass. My friends were all dumbfounded and looking at me like, 'What the fuck...?' while probably also thinking, 'Let's see how this turns out...' Well, I knew I was hurt, but there was no way I was going to cry in front of my friends or Father Arthur. So once again, I was going to be a tough guy (a.k.a., a moron), and I repeated the same thing to Father Arthur, "When I get big, I'm going to beat you up." He again answered, "Don't wait till you get big, if you have to do something, do it now." So yet again I took the bait... and leave of my senses, running up the bleachers for him to again kick me down those bleachers, choking back my tears even harder this time when I landed on my already aching ass again. But stupidity will always prevail, so, ONE MORE TIME WITH GUSTO and my voice quivering, I repeated to Father Arthur, *"When I get big, I'm going to beat you up."* Of course, by this point I was really hoping my friends would hold me back, but NOPE, they watched this ship get shot down for a third time because to no one's surprise, like the bigger bully he was, Father Arthur repeated his answer, "Don't wait till you get big, if you have to do something, do it now!" There I went, back up the bleachers, but this time I thought I'd out-thug him and side-step his kick, which gave him the opportunity to show his versatility by getting me in a head-lock and throwing me down the bleachers instead of kicking me (*I think he had more practice at this than me…*). Even though I was stuck on stupid, my friends finally had mercy on me to physically stop me from going at Father Arthur again because they saw nothing good coming from this record continuing to skip, so they pulled me out of the gym. Thank God because I might have broken into a hundred pieces if I bounced down those bleachers another time.

We knew we couldn't get at Father Arthur directly, but we tried to cook up a plan to kill his dog, a boxer – **LISTEN!** I know what you're thinking. Well, this was the neighborhood we grew up in, if you couldn't get at the person directly, you went after something close to them. We were a bunch of thug kids in grammar school who didn't have any sense or understanding; we had a lot to learn. Fortunately, some one of us had sense enough to think better of our plan to hurt an innocent animal, but we kept trying to think of something else we could do directly to Father Arthur to get back at him. And think about it: we didn't call Father Arthur the hoodlum priest for nothing because he was a street kid like us, which meant he was always two steps ahead of us, and anyway, he was better at this game than we were.

In spite of it all, I got out of grammar school without ever getting revenge on Father Arthur, and I started hanging out in Red Hook instead of South Brooklyn when I was in high school. Red Hook was a different neighborhood even though it was right next to South Brooklyn with lots of similarities between the two, just with different people. But just like South Brooklyn back then, 90% of the people in Red Hook were Italian, related to each other, living for generations in the same place and was an Italian ghetto. When I was about 23, I came back from college on a break and I decided to go to the bazaar for a feast of some saint at my parish. I hadn't seen Father Arthur since I was about 14 years old and at this point I was about 220 lbs, playing linebacker for my college football team. Believe it or not, I used him as a reference on my application when I applied to the Catholic college I went away to, and yes, he gladly gave me a good reference. So Father Arthur was at a table selling raffles. I patiently waited in line for a raffle and I hear, "Next." Father Arthur looks up at me, then looks down, up, then down and up again (he did a double, then triple take), then says, "Lenny, is that you?" In my best Slip Mahoney/Leo Gorcey from the Bowery Boys voice, I say, "Yeah fadder, it's me." Father Arthur looks at me and says, "Boy, you got big!" Still staying in the Bowery Boys' character, I say, "You think you can kick the shit out of me now?" He looks both ways to make sure no one else was listening, then at me and says, "Go down to the back stairwell where the bowling alleys are [how many of you remember the bowling alleys in our grammar school?], and I'll be right behind you." My answer to him was, "Bullshit! So you can kick me down the stairs like you did when I was a kid." He answered me, "Not only did you get big, you got smart." I went around the table with a big smile on my face, tears in my eyes, I hugged him with all my might and said, "Thank you Father. Thank you for everything you did for me." In this case, these were tears of joy, not the tears of rage from when I was a punk kid.

Frequent Flying

My friend Patty went to a Cat-lic (that's the way we pronounced Catholic) grammar school where this nun used to rant and rave all the time that she'd traveled all around the world, but now she "was stuck in Red Hook with all you hoodlums!" Patty told me how, again, nuns being what they were back then, had no compassion; she was hitting him for who knows what reason (they never seemed to need a reason). So, Patty said he was trying to get away from her by running around the classroom until she cornered him where the only thing near him was the class globe. So in response to her repeated complaint about being stuck in Red Hook with hoodlums after traveling the world, he picked up the globe and threw it at her, yelling, "You wanna see the world?? Here it is!!" Needless to say, Patty was immediately expelled from his Catholic school and wound up in public school for showing that nun... that he'd have *none* of that.

Say Cheese!

I had a cousin we called _Ralphie Boc,_ who was an out-and-out lunatic. My uncle married Ralphie's older sister, so we called each other cousins. Anyway, some kid (I don't know what the kid's name was) owed Ralphie money; it could have been a quarter, it could have been a dollar, whatever it was, I don't know. Well, despite being a nutjob, Ralphie also had a reasonable side. He was the type that if the kid just told Ralphie that he didn't have the money, Ralphie would have been fine with that. But Nooooooooo! This kid kept blowing smoke up Ralphie's ass, telling him that he'd give Ralphie the money later, and later and later, but never giving Ralphie a red cent. Ralphie said he felt like the kid was making a jerk-off out of him and decided it was time to act. So what did Ralphie do? He waited outside the kid's house one day and when the kid came down the stairs of his stoop, Ralphie sucker-punched the kid in the face making the kid fall back. Then Ralphie jumped on top of the kid to hold him down, pulled a pair of plyers out of his pocket, pried the kid's mouth open, then ripped out one of the kid's teeth. Ralphie got off the kid and then ran down the block waving around the plyers that had the other kid's tooth dripping blood in its grip. I'm sure you're wondering what happened after that. Remember where I came from, no one went to the cops, and 'people who knew people' intervened. When everything came to a head, "people" heard how the kid owed Ralphie money and was dogging Ralphie, which made them agree the kid was making a jerk-off out of Ralphie, so they sided with Ralphie which meant nothing was done about the kid losing the tooth. Unfortunately, and maybe it's not surprising, Ralphie is one of my cousins who is no longer with us because he got shot.

LANGUAGE: BROOKLYN SAYINGS – NO, NOT "YOUR MUTHA"

UNIQUE NEW YORK... *BROOKLYN*!

Coming from Brooklyn, our language and pronunciations of words is different than the other boroughs, but I'm not sure a non-New Yorker can really hear the difference. And even though they do a really good job at it, we've all seen when people from other northeastern states (I won't name names here) and even sometimes from other countries are cast in the role of someone from Brooklyn on some of these cop shows. You'll also see that there are different sayings, slang terms, euphemisms or colloquialisms (how's that Blair??!), to say the same thing. Other boroughs and beyond may also stake claims to some of the same sayings and similar ways of saying these same things, but I heard them in Brooklyn, so I'm claiming them **for** Brooklyn and I hope I don't upset anyone for saying some things a little differently.

So let's talk about Brooklynese, which is our own sub-dialect of American English. If you came from Brooklyn during certain eras, like when I was growing up, maybe till the 1990s and a little beyond, you'd know *the Brooklyn Alphabet*: Fuckin-Aaaa, Fuckin-Beee, Fuckin-Ceee, but it goes beyond just throwing the word "fuck" in front of another word or phrase. Like sometimes, instead of going, "Um" or "You know" while you're trying to think of what to say next, some of us used to say, "fuckin." For example, "When we were going to the store... fuckin... this guy came over to us and asked for a ride." We had a vulgar eloquence in how we spoke. We talked "street." Brooklynites are also known to put the word "but" at the end of a sentence, like, "That's a nice car, but." Proper sentence structure was of no concern for us. Another thing, if we want to get someone's attention, instead of calling them by their name, we called out; "A!" or "O!" I'm a swim coach and even now, when I want to get the attention of any of my kids, when I yell out, "A!" or "O!", the kid I'm yelling to knows to turn around. Isn't that great!! But I think the best-known example of Brooklynese is how we change the "th" sound to a "d" sound, like "dese" instead of "these." And don't forget replacing "thr" with "tr" – like saying "tread" instead of "thread." To be sure we include the whole kit and kaboodle, we'll say, *"Dis, dat* and *de odher ding..."* (how's that Mallor?). Like I said earlier, to make this book readable to more than just people from Brooklyn, I'm not going to word everything phonetically. 'K? Anyway, just remember, this is not some research work from a historian or a linguist, just a regular guy telling it like I lived it.

Again, I may ramble on at times, but stay with me here 'cause here we go!

Describing People Who Get Blood From Stones
Tighter than a crab's ass, and that's water-proof
S/He's so cheap, you can hear 'em squeak
S/He don't go for spit
S/He don't go for corks
S/He has alligator arms
S/He has short arms and long pockets
S/He still has their baptism money
Getting money out of them is like squeezing blood from a stone or a rock
When s/he opens his/her wallet, moths come out
Chintzy, cheapskate, penny-pincher

When I was a kid and I asked for money, I would get told, "When the eagle shits..." Which is when someone gets paid.

It's Just As Good As Money	
Fazooles Schkaroles Cabbage Dough Scratch Bread Mullah	Money
C-Note Yard	$100
½ Yard	$50

It's Just As Good As Money	
Fin Pound Saw-buck	$5
Bone Bean	$1
Two Bits	25 cents
The big nickel	A quarter coin
Paid In Spades Paid Through the Nose Went for My Lungs Too Dear Lost my shirt Jipped Ripped off	Too expensive, robbed, gouged
Got It For A Song	Got it cheap
S/He made out like a bandit	Someone who got a really good deal, made a lot of money, or who's in a really good situation
S/He made a score	Someone made a lot of money
Hit Me Up Front me	Someone asked to borrow money, but you never got it back
Money grubber	Someone who panhandles or begs for money
Taking It On the Chin	Taking a loss
Money down the drain	Wasting money
What do you think money grows on trees?	Someone who spends a lot of money
What is it wood?	When someone is owed money, they might ask, "what is it, wood?" - it's almost like, 'forget about it…' But nothing else is like 'forget about it'
Easy Mark	Someone who is easy to swindle

It's Just As Good As Money	
Hot Swag Fell Off A Truck	Stolen
G & R / Grab and run Five finger discount	Stealing
They're lining their pockets	People who are stealing
You sit next to the door at a restaurant to...	Dine and dash – run out without paying
He's A Sport Has a hole in his/her pocket Money burns a hole in his pocket	Likes to spend money
They gave away the store	They gave away everything for nothing or really cheaply
Jack-shit	Nothing at all
On the Balls Of His Ass Doesn't Have Two Nickels To Rub Together Doesn't Have A Pot to Piss In, Or A Window to Throw It Out of	Broke, no money
Grease some palms	Pay off or bribe someone to do something for you
If I had your money, I'd burn mine	Telling someone that they have a lot of money: A Tommy Mo saying!
He has more money than God	Now, I was brought up with Irish nuns and Italian priests; we got taught that Jesus, God's son, had nothing but his preaching and the clothes on his back (robes and sandals) - So, I would think if God had money, wouldn't he leave it to His son? So I do not know where that saying came from, and it always bothers me to this day when I hear someone say it

It's Just As Good As Money

Send it in Bet the farm Sure thing Five will get you ten I'll bet you dollars to donuts...	Betting everything you have on something because you have that much confidence in the outcome
Fork it over	Give it over
Sponge	Free-loader, parasite Someone known for puttin' on the feed bag

Starting To End

From the Jump / from Jump Street Out Of the Gate Got in on the ground floor Post time (Tony 59 used to say this one)	From the beginning
Put the kabash or Kaybash on something Pack it in	Put an end to something
Calling it a day	The end of something

Just Say The Word

Keep It Under Wraps Don't Let On Keep them in the dark	Keep something quiet or a secret
Nix Deep Six	Cancel something, drop a matter, stop talking about something
Spill It Quit Stalling	Stop delaying in telling something
Motor mouth Can't get a word in edgewise Won't come up for air	Someone who won't stop talking
Don't put your two cents in	Stay out of something, or mind your own business

Just Say The Word	
Bite the bullet Put a lid on it Put a sock in it Zip it Shut your trap	Keep your mouth shut, keep quiet, shut up
In one ear and out the other In one ear and out the same	Someone who is not listening
You don't listen, you just don't listen	What I say to my son to this day!
Pay No Mind List What am I, wood?	Ignoring someone or being ignored
What do I look like, Claude Reins?	Being ignored like the invisible man
Is Your Hand Stuck In A Bowling Ball	Why didn't you call on the telephone? These days, why didn't you text or IM me?
Thrown A Curve Ball	Changed the rules unexpectedly
You Got Some Line of Shit/bullshit	Bullshit, lies
Bullshit makes flowers grow, [insert name] makes them over-flow	Sung to someone who's a big liar
You lie like a Persian rug, Sir Lie A Lot Stand on the table When this one talks, the boots don't help	Someone who lies and lies Sometimes when someone's a notorious bullshitter, you're just better off standing on a table, forget everything else
You're full of shit	A real Brooklynite won't say you're full of 'crap' to mean you're lying...
That's a lot of malarky	Lots of bullshit

Just Say The Word

You got more excuses than Carter has liver pills	Bullshitting, excuse-making	 How many of you remember Carter's Little Liver Pills? http://creativecommons.org/licenses/by/4.0/
Something doesn't hold water / Has too many holes		Unbelievable or not credible
Someone got buffaloed		They were fooled/bullshitted
Doesn't miss a trick		Someone who is aware and not much get passed him/her You can also be sarcastic with this, like saying someone is as sharp as a butter knife

Just Say The Word	
Tell the truth and shame the devil	What the nuns said to us when they wanted to get us to fess up about something that happened – a few of us in our class told the truth once and got hit really bad – after that, when they said tell us to "tell the truth and shame the devil," we lied like champs or like Persian rugs... because the moral of the story was we would get hit for telling the truth or for lying, so why not lie like you were going to get hit anyway??? At least you came upon the beatin honestly... Every so often in our lives, you'd get caught, or you'd catch a beating – It was part of growing up in our neighborhood
Cross my heart and hope to die; stick a needle in your eye I swear on my parents I swear on my kids	Swearing that you're telling the truth or will keep a confidence I HATE when people say they swear on their kids! To me, that's usually someone who's honesty is doubtful
Make no bones about it	To be frank or honest about something
Does a bear shit in the woods?	What you say when telling someone that it's a foregone conclusion that something is the truth
Come clean	Tell the truth/don't bullshit me/us

Just Say The Word	
Called on the carpet	Needing to explain oneself
Rat Squealer Snitch Stool pigeon Cheese eater	Someone who names names
Ratting Someone Out Throw Someone Under the Bus Drop a dime on someone Give someone up Sold out Finger someone Loose lips, sink ships	Calling the cops on someone, let someone else take the blame, betraying a confidence, telling on someone
Pinched	Having been arrested, being locked up
By the skin of one's teeth	Just barely made it
Playing D and D Don't Know Nuthin Dumb like a fox You have to be smart to play dumb	Pretend you don't understand when someone asks you a question by answering with "Who?", "What?", "When?", "Where?" and "Why?" never giving a straight answer Playing deaf and dumb
Something was laid out / making the case for something	Arguing your side of a case or making something clear
Don't pull any punches	Be straight-forward; just come right out and say something
How'd you make out?	What was the outcome?
Let's have it Lay it on me Give me the goods	Tell me what happened
Rigged up	A predetermined outcome
Sure as shit	Definitely, for sure

Just Say The Word	
Catch Wind Of Something Did you pick up on that?	Found out or heard about something Did you hear what I heard, or are you aware of what happened or was said?
On The Up And Up S/He's on the level Walking two feet in one shoe Walking on eggs Walking the straight and narrow	The truth, credible, being truthful
In the ball park	Not too far off, but needs more explanation
You bet your sweet ass	That is correct!
What are you driving at?	What do you mean, what are you trying to say?
God made all men, Louisville made them all equal	The way to even the physical odds because if you had a Louisville Slugger bat, you would be equal to almost anyone (Richie R.)
You know what I'm saying? You know what I mean? Catch my drift?	Do you understand?
It's on the tip of my tongue	I can't remember something
Half passed the cow's ass, a quarter to his balls Time to get a watch	When someone asked "what time is it?"

What's Your Name Again (*... So I Can Forget*)?	
Yo!	Calling someone without using a name, Or greeting someone

What's Your Name Again (*... So I Can Forget*)?	
Man	Instead of "pal" or "friend" or "buster," someone might say, "Look, man!" Or, "Oh, man! Could you believe that??" Then there's "The Man" when referring to the government or someone in authority that came into heavy use in the 1950s and 1960s by beatniks and hippies/the counter-culture
Dude	Another way of calling to someone without saying their name – replacing "buster" or "fellow" or "guy" – Used a lot in the 1960s – but before that, it was a term in the late 1800s referring to a fancy-dressed man, or a "dandy," a "city slicker"
Play ball	Cooperate with someone
Playing hardball	Not cooperating
I'm game, or someone else is game	I'm for it, or someone else is for doing something
Fair to Midland	S/He's ok
S/He's a pisser, goofball, clown	That person is very funny
Fuck you and the horse you rode in on! Go shit in your hat! Fuck em where they breathe	Really telling someone off or letting them know you are really pissed off at them, or how pissed you are at someone else
Someone is fit to be tied	They're really pissed off
Someone woke up on the wrong side of the bed This person has a burr under their saddle (Kansas saying)	Someone is in a bad mood or pissed off
Bone of contention	Something you have against someone else or something that's bothering you
Straighten someone out	Correcting someone, verbally or physically

What's Your Name Again (... *So I Can Forget*)?	
Your ass is grass! Also; Your ass is grass, and your mouth's a lawnmower, so start chopping!	Threatening someone for some perceived or real slight...
Kick ass and take names Kick ass and take no hostages	Football term used by the guys in the huddle
S/He is a good egg Piece of bread Bruzhute (prosciutto) Banana Meatball Salami Bacalao	A nice or good person, someone you could fuck with – remember, Italians associate food with goodness!
You're a drag	Someone who makes people feel bad or at least is boring
Just because you can, doesn't mean you should	Good advice!
Hey, numbnuts	A friendly way of calling someone stupid
If stupid was electricity, you would be a power light house You're as sharp as a butter knife/cue ball	You're really stupid
Someone took that hook, line and sinker	Someone who's stupid or gullible
Don't look at me in that tone of voice	Someone who is looking at you with a confused look, or a nasty look or a look you just don't like
Mamo(One of my brother's favorite sayings), Imbecile/ Imbo (Another of my brother's favorite sayings) Hey fucko Chooch or Jootch You don't know shit from shine-ola	Calling someone a dope

What's Your Name Again (... *So I Can Forget*)?	
Smarten up Take your head out of your ass	Don't be such a dope
The lights are on, but nobody's home The elevator doesn't go to the top floor Sharp as a butter knife Sharp as a bowling ball A few bricks shy of a load A few sandwiches shy of a picnic Not the sharpest tool in the shed If fish is good brain food, you should eat a whale	No brains, not very bright
Fat fuck	Insulting someone that you don't like, whether they're fat or not
Rat bastard (said as 'rat basted')	Another way to call someone a scumbag
Messing around Fooling around Fucking around	Kidding around
Fat bastard (said, 'fat basted')	Sign of affection toward someone you're kidding around with – and yes, there is a difference (right Eddie?!)
Get off your high horse Don't think who the hell you are Don't be full of yourself What? Your shit don't stink?	Learn humility
I'm doing this with my glasses on, so I can look intelligent (again, right Eddie?!)	Self-deprecating humor
S/He got themselves into some jackpot/pickle	They got into a bad situation or in deep trouble

What's Your Name Again (... *So I Can Forget*)?	
Do me a solid Call it in	When you want someone to do you a favor
Throw them a bone	You're going to do someone else a favor Or doing something/just enough for someone to stop them from complaining
Return the favor	Paying someone back (could be good or bad)
Someone asks: "What are you looking at?" Response: "I don't know I'm trying to figure that out"	Calling someone ugly – and a nice way to wind up in a fight
Tapping that	Fooling around with someone – usually when talking about a guy fooling around with a girl
Glad eye	Looking at someone in a flirty way
Making time with him/her	Getting intimate with a guy or a girl
Going steady They're/We're an item	Dating someone long-term
Keeping company with someone	Usually, old-timers would say this when they were dating someone
Keeping someone – keeping a guy or keeping a girl	When you're acting as sugar mamma or sugar daddy for someone you're fooling around with – no marriage – You're paying their bills
They're tight	When people are really close
Stood up	Someone who doesn't show up for a date
It's quits!	Young people said this when they were breaking up with each other
Hump and dump	When someone fools around/has sex with someone, then breaks off any relationship with them right after
If a girl had an ankle bracelet on her left ankle, it meant she had a boyfriend	In those days, no one was up-front about relationships unless they were straight Everyone else kept them under wraps

What's Your Name Again (... *So I Can Forget*)?	
Your mother's like a doorknob; everyone gets a turn	Calling someone's mother a loose woman
Choking the chicken Spanking the monkey	Terms for masturbation, or jerking off....
Your mother wears combat boots!	Telling someone their mother is masculine
Stick it or shove it up your ass Put it where the sun don't shine	Telling someone that you don't like what they're offering
All bets are off	No rules; anything goes
Up your nose with a rubber hose! Go jump in a lake Up your hole with a mellow roll	A funny way to tell someone to go to hell – came from the program "Welcome Back Kotter"
Up your ass with a piece of glass!	Another way to tell someone to go to hell
Go scratch your ass with a broken bottle	One more way to tell someone to go to hell
Take off your mask, Halloween is over	Calling someone ugly
Sticks and stones may break my bones, but words/names will never harm me But when I die, I'll spit in your eye for all the names you called me	The way to answer people who are saying mean things to you
You're so low you could play handball off a street curb You're lower than a snake's stomach	Another rank-out, calling someone a low-life
When you were born, your mother said, "What a treasure! Your father said, "Let's burry it..."	You're so ugly...

What's Your Name Again (... *So I Can Forget*)?	
Almost don't count, except for horseshoes and hand grenades	How do you answer someone who tells you that something almost happened or they are almost done doing something
Hump/Humpo	Sign of affection, a friendly insult, a term of endearment – most of the time
Size him/her up Check him/her out	Looking someone over, trying to figure them out
Someone is fishing or on a fishing expedition	Someone is trying to figure something out, to guess
On the fence It can go one way or the other	Not sure about someone or something
So quiet you could hear a pin/ feather drop	It's very quiet
Beef	A problem, as in having a beef with someone
Keep your mother off the streets, and I won't be a mother fucker	-When someone calls you a mother fucker!
If it wasn't for us dicks, you scumbags wouldn't be in business	-When someone calls you a dick
Jerk-off Douche bag Hoople Asshole Dirt-bag Motherfucker Motherless Motherfucker (*inspired by my wife's uncle) Dick Scumbag Skell Clown Mutt	Insults telling someone they're stupid or a low-life
Learning about the birds and the bees	Learning about the facts of life, usually about how babies are made

What's Your Name Again (... *So I Can Forget*)?	
Don't be fresh Don't be smart Keep your nose clean Stop fucking around Knock it off	Don't be disrespectful, behave
Oh, for crying out loud! Holy shit!	Unreal, I can't believe it
I'm gonna eat em up! I'm gonna suck the air outta them!	Usually, what someone says about a baby to show how much they love them
Big time!	Agreement

How *YOU* Doin!	
Jake (that's what I called my old roommate)	Everything is ok
On egg shells Walking two feet in one shoe Sweating bullets On pins and needles Like a long-tailed cat in a room full of rocking chairs Handle with kid gloves Shit a pill Shit a brick Shit my pants Scare the piss out of me Boogie man	Concerned or nervous, be careful; something to be afraid of
Keep your shirt on Don't get your panties/underwear all in a bunch Don't Get Your Nickers In A Twist Hold your horses Don't have a hairy canary	Relax, don't get upset/flip out, wait
Step on it / If you go any slower, you'll be going backward	Speed it up, you're going too slow
Put the squeeze on someone Put the screws to someone Lean on someone	Putting pressure on someone or trying to hurt someone
Put someone on the spot	Putting pressure on someone to make a tough decision

How *YOU* Doin!	
Roll over	Giving into someone or something, disclosing a secret
Making or starting a scene S/he could start a fight in a peace conference	Someone who makes lots of trouble
Taking someone under their wing	Teaching or mentoring someone or protecting them
Someone got the green light	They got the ok or clearance to move forward or do something
Giving someone a pass	Letting someone go, don't hurt them, believe their bullshit
We copped our way out of it	We bullshitted our way out of it
Egg someone on	Encourage someone, usually not in a good way
Going to work on someone Pow, bang, bing Ba-ta-bing Throw em a beating S/He caught a beating Take a beating Knock your block off	Hitting someone
Cruising for a bruising Aching for a breaking	Someone who's looking to get hit
Shit's on It's time to get down Let's get down	You're fighting another gang (we, the Little Gents, had 'shit's on' with our rivals, the Sinclairs)
We're going down	We're having a fight

How *YOU* Doin!

I'm going to teach you, and then I'm going to lose you	Someone who is not paying attention
Does that suit you?	Is that ok, or do you like that?
Nione He ate that sandwich like a nione Like nobody's business	Something fast or something you really like, or you get a kick out of (am I right, Rider?)
To beat the band Like a champ Like it's going out of style	Extensive, similar to nione
Take the high road	Don't argue; let the other person think they're right, no need to confirm (Ed Cooper)
Make good	Take responsibility
Have at it	Go ahead, do it
Shut Eye	Sleeping
Step On It	Speed It Up
Give Them The Air	Ignore, don't pay attention to someone
Give Someone The Slip Ditch them	Getting rid of someone, leaving them
Hot boot in the ass	Kick someone in the ass, telling them to get lost
Play Ball	Cooperate

How *YOU* Doin!

Pocket pool	When a guy has his hands in his pocket, and you're not sure what he's doing, maybe playing a little "pocket pool" with the family jewels
One hand washes the other, then both hands wash the face, and that's how you stay clean	Taking care of business
All right for you If you say so	The response to someone who doesn't believe you or with whom you disagree

Don't Let The Door Hit You In The Ass...

Scram
Beat it
Put an egg in your shoe and beat it
Take a powder
Get lost
Hit the road
Make like a tree and leave
Don't go away mad, just go away
Make yourself scarce
Put them on the pay-no-mind-list
Give someone the slip
Go see where you gotta go
Go play in traffic
Go take a long walk off a short pier
Don't break balls

Don't Let The Door Hit You In The Ass...	
Why don't you go chase yourself around the block	My late 93-year-old mother-in-law's way of telling someone to leave her alone or to get lost!

Seeing Where We Gotta Go...	
S/He's not Magellan	Someone who's not good with directions
It's not around the corner	Which means... it's far away...
S/He lives around my way	Someone who lives nearby or in my neighborhood
Heads up!	Telling someone to look up because something may be in the air and about to hit them – personally, I think we should tell people to cover their heads, not look up to get hit in the face...
S/He drives like a cowboy or a hack	Someone who takes chances driving fast like a cowboy or a taxi driver
Taking a header Ass over tea kettle Head over heels	Someone who fell head-first
Shake a leg	Hurry up
Tear ass	Run fast
Bum's rush	Either rushing someone out the door, like a bum Or When you rush toward someone/something, like when it's general admission at a concert, everyone is rushing to get to the front of the venue, in front of the stage
Flat-leaver	Someone who leaves you high and dry

Seeing Where We Gotta Go...	
Coming out of the woodwork	Things or people are coming from every direction
In the clink On the road In stir In college Up the river In the can	In jail

You're Stylin!	
What did you get your ears lowered? You broke the barber's window	Did you get a haircut?
Is there a flood? Did you get those pants in the year of the flood? Why don't you have a party and invite your pants down to meet your shoes	Your pants are too high
Want to get rid of 10 pounds of ugly fat? Cut off your head You are so ugly; you look like you got hit with a bag full of nickels and were waiting for change If my dog had a face like yours, I'd shave his ass and make him walk backwards S/He is so ugly, s/he has to sneak up on a glass or water You're so ugly that when you were born, the doctor slapped your mother instead of your ass! I have a good match, my ass and your face What a face, what a figure, two more legs, and you'll look like trigger A Face Only A Mother Could Love	You're ugly
Double-bagger	Someone so ugly that you both wear bags over your heads, in case the ugly person's bag falls off, they don't know what *you* look like

86

You're Stylin!

So and so looks like a rag-picker	Someone who is not dressed well, is sloppy, or clothes are disheveled
The horse got out of the stable Your fly is open	The zipper on your pants is undone
Pissing like a racehorse	Someone who is going to the bathroom all the time – usually a guy
Ashes to ashes, dust to dust, what's an underwear without a crust?	Someone who's dirty

Is This Humerus Or Did I Just Hit My Funny Bone?

Face	See "you're ugly" under the "grooming" table
Puss	Face
Pickle-puss	Someone with a sour face
Angels with dirty faces	What the nuns said to us when we did something wrong to try and make us feel guilty (also a great movie)
Trombone, schnozz I know this may be gross, but when someone has a lot of phlegm and they spit it out, we called that gerb	Nose (yes Mark...)
Doors	Ears
Gams	Legs, usually referring to women
Dogs	Feet
Dogs Are Barking	Feet are hurting
You need to go to blacksmith for shoes	Big feet
Guns	Muscular arms

Is This Humerus Or Did I Just Hit My Funny Bone?	
Family jewels	Genitalia, usually the male's
S/He has a gun	S/He has a good throwing arm
Someone is full of piss and vinegar	Usually, when referring to a woman
S/He is a 22 Crazy as a bedbug Batshit crazy Apeshit Nuts	Someone who's a little crazy (Uncle Shorty)
This one can't walk and chew gum at the same time	Someone who's not coordinated
S/He got a wild hair up their ass	Someone went a little crazy or did something out of the ordinary
S/He is big-boned Baby Huey	A nicer way of saying someone is fat
Kisser	Mouth
Stringbean Skinny balink Tall drink of water	Someone who's really skinny

Also Ran	
Flatfoot Bull Heat John Law The Man Fuzz	Names for police
He's A Pill Stick in the mud	Someone unpleasant
S/He favors you S/He's A Dead Ringer Cut Off His/Her Head	Someone who looks like you

Also Ran	
Schem MamaLuke (Albert's and Sean's favorite saying) Lame Boob Sap	Dumb
'What Do You Think, I Just Fell Off the Turnip Truck?'	Do you think I'm a dope?
Don't Get Cute Don't be a wisenheimer	Don't be a smart-ass
Busted Ass Stepped In Shit Has A Horseshoe Up One's Ass You got it made in the shade	Lucky
I can't win for losing	Really unlucky
Up against it Behind the 8-ball	Having a hard time, usually having to do with money
Hit the Nail On the Head	Got it exactly right
From The Year Of The Flood That went out with the flood	Really old (insinuating from Noah's time)
Short Fuse	bad or quick temper
Dead As A Door Nail	Lifeless, done
Hands down That's all she wrote	It's done
Piss and Vinegar	Full of life, ornery
Lollipop Cucumber Bick-A-Keel (bastardized Italian for cucumber or lollipop)	Hen-pecked, sucker
Hot Shit	Funny or incredible
I Dig It Can you dig it? (Remember that line in "The Warriors?"	I like it, I understand it Can you understand?
It's his/her bag	Something that someone likes
Can Eat Off the Floor	Very clean

Also Ran

Stand Up Guy/Girl Straightshooter	Someone you can count on, reliable, honest
S/He's good people	A good person
Barking Up The Wrong Tree	Wrong person, assumption, idea
In Cahoots	Colluding, conspiring
On The Ball	Smart, knows what's going on
In His Pocket On the Take	Being bribed, dependent financially or under someone's influence
You Broke The Barber's Window	You need a hair cut
He Has More Money Than God... As Far As I Know, God Had No Money	Very wealthy From the belief that Jesus was God and a poor carpenter
He's Tighter Than A Clam's Ass, And That's Water Proof S/He Still Has Her/His Communion Money Don't Go For Spit/Corks Short Arms, Long Pockets Alligator arms	Very cheap
Champaign Taste With Beer Pockets	Can't manage money
Right Up My Alley	Something you like
No Shit Sherlock No shit Dick Tracey	Yeah, I know
S/He's A Ringer	Too old to play a sport or secretly a professional
So, who died and made you King/Boss? who died and left you in charge?	Someone who is bossy
A refrigerator with a head on top	Someone really big
God made all men, and Louisville made them all equal The Italian equalizer	The answer to dealing with a tough-guy Baseball bat

Also Ran

Chief cook and bottle washer	Someone who does everything
It's colder than a witches tit, doing push-ups in the snow	It's really cold outside
Birds of a feather flock together Two peas in a pod	People who are alike
The apple doesn't fall far from the tree	Someone who looks or is like a parent
So and so is a piece of work	Someone who's a character or kind of shady
Lick it off the grass	It didn't come out of nowhere

Breaking Balls

Let someone walk away a good distance from you and then call them back over. Once they come back, you ask them, "Hey, where would you be if I didn't call you?"
Two guys would run up to another guy, and each would get on a side of the third guy. The guy on the left would say, "Left ball!" The guy on the right would immediately say, "Right ball!" Then, together, they'd say, "Who's that prick in the middle?!" My friends *Sal-Tunnel-Tooth* and *Jimmy-Rocks* were the best at this! The guy in the middle would usually push the other two guys away and yell at them, "Get the fuck outta here!"
Is that good? (99% of people will say, 'yes'), then stick it up your ass, good things don't hurt!
Did you get those shoes from Buster Brown (shoe store)? -- because they are busted on the bottom and brown on top.
Did you get those clothes from Robert Hall? Robert threw them out, and you hauled them in.
You lie like a Persian rug
Hey, you want a job putting diapers on pissclams?
Hey, Love Boat! Not you, Shipwreck!! (usually said by a girl to a guy)

Breaking Balls	
Why don't you have a party and invite your pants to meet your shoes! High waters	Your pants are short
Get Outta Here/Get the *fuck* outta here You Gotta Be Kiddin Fugettaboutit I'm not buying it	No way, unbelievable
Not For Nothing Not For Anything	Incidentally
I'm Just Saying	Not trying to insult or I might be wrong, but...
My ass and your face! Or My fart and your breath!	The response when someone asks for a match

Rhyme Time and Kids Tunes	
Oh.... How I hate to get up in the morning Oh.... How I love to stay in be-e-e-ed	This is what I used to sing to my sister to wake her up
Whistle while you work Hitler was a jerk Mussolini pulled his weenie Now it doesn't work	This was something we picked up, probably a pro-Allies propaganda rhyme to show support for the desired outcome of WWII
It's raining, it's pouring The old man is snoring He went to bed and bumped his head And he couldn't get up in the morning	This is basically a nursery rhyme that most of us only knew the first verse
A tisket, a tasket, a green and yellow basket I wrote a letter to my mother And on the way, I dropped it	This was something else that either was or became a song. Some people say "... a green and yellow basket," others say "... a brown and yellow basket." The song by Ella Fitzgerald said, "... a brown and yellow basket."

Rhyme Time and Kids Tunes	
Oh, where have you been, Billy boy, Billie boy Oh, where have you been, charming Billy I've been to see my wife, she's a joy of all my life She's a young thing and cannot leave her mother Did she bake a cherry pie, Billie boy, Billie Boy Did she bake a cherry pie, charming Billie Yes, she baked a cherry pie with a twinkle in her eye She's a young thing and cannot leave her mother Did she take your hat and coat, Billie boy, Billie boy Did she take your hat and coat, charming Billie Yes, she took my hat and coat, but she gave it to the goat She's a young thing and cannot leave her mother	A little creepy by today's standards, but this was one of those songs we found ourselves randomly singing
1-2-3, get off my father's apple tree	The introduction to playing a hiding game
Poor little [so and so] sitting on a fence Trying to make $1 out of 99 cents	In my neighborhood, this was just a saying – for my wife, it was a rhyme to repeat and start counting from 1 while someone was jumping rope
Lenny and Sophie sitting in a tree K-I-S-S-I-N-G First comes love Then comes marriage Then comes Lenny in a baby carriage Sucking his thumb Wetting his pants Doing the hoola, hoola, hoola dance	A rhyme to tease someone when it's discovered they have a crush on someone by naming the two of them in the song

Rhyme Time and Kids Tunes	
This little piggy went to market (pull the big toe) This little piggy stayed home (pull the second toe) This little piggy had roast beef (pull the third toe) This little piggy had none (pull the fourth toe) And this little piggy said, wee, wee, wee, all the way home (pull the pinky toe)	When you want to tickle a kid's feet
My father is the butcher My mother cuts the meat And I'm the little meatball that runs around the street	A general rhyme to have kids sing when you know they're mischievous
My father is the dentist My mother is the nurse I'm the little toothache that hurts and hurts and hurts	See the one above
Shave and a haircut, two bits Oh, and a ladder, bullshit!	Don't ask; I have no idea what this was about
Lulu had a baby She named him Tiny Tim Put him in the piss pot To learn him how to swim He swam to the bottom He swam to the top Lulu got disgusted and pulled him by his... Cocktail, ginger ale, five cents a glass If you don't like it, shove it up your... Holy Moses, King of the Jews Wipes his ass with the Daily News	This was the kind of thing we mindlessly spouted back then

NICKNAMES

A LITTLE BACKGROUND

I was going to make two completely different chapters; one with a list of nicknames and the other with all the stories about people from my neighborhood, including those with nicknames. But my wife said when there's a story about somebody with a nickname, I should tell them together because it'll help people get to know better who everyone was or is when they read their stories. For example, _Anthony Moose's_ nickname and the story about him not wanting to eat Chinese food ...because the Japanese bombed Pearl Harbor... you gotta tell that together, or you'll lose the whole feel for him; it's like separating peas from carrots! Separating the stories from people with nicknames might mean we'd have to use footnotes, cross-referencing, or something else fancy, so instead, this is how I'm doing it in this chapter, "NICKNAMES" with the stories about people with nicknames together. Isn't that nice?

Now, I know sometimes people get upset when someone else talks about what happened with them way back then and in mentioning their nicknames, and we all know that some nicknames were unkind, to say the least. Well, I'm not trying to upset or shame anyone with this chapter or anything else, but these nicknames are what people were known as when we were kids, and again, I'm just telling it like I remember it. You gotta also realize that having people around us giving and getting nicknames is another thing that makes us who we are. Let's be honest, there were nicknames for people when we were kids that no one would use for anyone today, for good reason. But just about all of us who lived in my neighborhood look back on these days with the same affection that I do, and we cherish those times. For the most part, my goal with this and the other chapters is to talk about fun things, and hopefully at no one else's expense, so I hope that's the way this comes across. On another point, for some people with nicknames, I don't know any stories and as a matter of fact, I might not have even met some of them. It just might be that

I **_only knew of_** them and their nicknames, and that was it. So if you don't see anything else except the nickname, that's why, SO DON'T ASK, my wife already did!

So, to earn a nick name, you might of been named for a body part. For example, "_Jerry Ears_" because his ears were big. Or you had a certain way about you, like "_Jimmy Psycho_" or "_Vinny the Loon_" – those names speak for themselves. You could've also been named for a color like "_Whitey_" – I think every neighborhood had a _"Whitey."_ You might've earned a nickname because of size; example, "_Frankie the Animal_" because he was tall and broad (he was a great softball player too). There are other people who have nicknames, and I don't know why, but I try to mention them, the best I can. Just as an FYI, most of the people I interacted with in these stories were Italian, unless otherwise noted, or unless I just don't know, in which case I _won't_ note it.

There were multiple people with the same nickname, but they might of come from different neighborhoods. I'll give you an example that's close to home for me: my father was known as _Joe Monk_ and my friend _Monkey's_ father was also _Joe Monk_. Then, there was _Smiley_ from Red Hook, and _Smiley_ from South Brooklyn – they both smiled a lot, how's about that? There were two guys called _Fishy_; one was from Third Aven and the other from Fifth Aven. And two _Bobby Bumps_, one from Third Aven and the other from DeGraw Street. There was a _Babes_ from Fifth Aven and a _Babes_ from Smith Street. Two guys were called _Sickness_ and two _Joey C._s – one of each was in the Gents and the Sinclairs. There were a few Bops, and I don't know why 'Bop.' One of the _Fishys'_ uncles was _John the Bop_. _Joe-Bop_ came from Red Hook. _Vinny-Bop_ and _Be-Bop_ were related and came from 5th Aven.

Some people didn't have nicknames, but we always called them by both their first and last names, which is kind of like having a nickname but minus the actual nickname. The most infamous and dear to our hearts was the one and only _Patty Burke_! You had to say both of their names for anyone to know who you were talking about.

Here We Go... Head Up! _Because Where Else Would You Start_?

Pregnant Head: His head was so big that it stood out and the only way to describe it was to compare it to a woman in her 9th month of pregnancy (...

she would've been *"very pregnant"*!). In the eighth grade, when we were in Sister Mary Malachy's class, *Pregnant Head* asked if the 'iron curtain' was really iron. Needless to say, he got the shit kicked out of him by Sister Mary Malachy, who was meaner than a barrel full of rattlesnakes. A week later, Sister Mary Malachy asked what was the most economical way to get to England from the U.S.? His answer? "Wait for the Atlantic Ocean to freeze and ice skate over." What happened next, you ask?? ... *Pregnant Head* got the shit kicked out of him!

Ten-Pound-Head: Another guy with a big head (see *Pregnant Head* and *Egghead*). When my father died, this short and stocky guy with ...a big head... came up to me, crying, and while he was hugging me, my Aunt Butchie quietly (we would have said, on the Q.T.), grabbed my attention and was mouthing to me that he was *Ten-Pound-Head*... I gotta tell you, it took a lot for me to keep from busting out laughing. The poor guy is commiserating with me about the death of my dad, telling me how much he loved him, and now I have this nickname rolling around in my head, knowing how well it fit! I knew him from the neighborhood and he was one of the nicest guys around, but until that moment, I had no idea that he was *Ten-Pound-Head*.

Blubberhead: Another nice guy from the neighborhood, and if I remember right, he was also a fruit peddler like so many of the men back then were, including my father and both grandfathers. Oh yeah, ... and he had a big head.

Barrel Head: Can you guess? Yes, a man who had a big head. I asked my friend Popeye if he knew anyone who could bartend at my first wedding and he introduced me to *Barrel Head*. To his credit, he was a very good bartender and a really nice guy.

Helium Head: One more big-headed guy... (see *Egghead*, *Pregnant Head*, *Cannonball* and *Ten-Pound-Head*). One of the guys who I knew of in my neighborhood.

Cannonball: Another guy, Sally, with a big head (see *Pregnant Head*). He looked like Lou Costello (of Abbott and Costello fame) and sounded just like him too! I just found out that *Cannonball* passed away not long ago.

Danny Football Head: Should be self-explanatory. My friend Louie G called him the Phantom because when we Lil' Gents were going to fight any other gang, Danny went all by himself to spy on them and report back to us. He was kind of a ninja.

Freddie Pinhead: He always had a crew-cut, so his head looked like it was covered with a bunch of pins. He lived around the corner from me and was a little older than me, so we didn't hang out.

Pusshead/Pizza-Face: Yes, this was not cool at all, it was cruel and downright mean. This guy had a bad case of acne. I guess you could argue that a good number of these nicknames were cruel, and although that's true, this was how it was back then. This was all normal to us and I'll say it again, I'm just telling it like I lived it.

Eagle Head: I have no idea why he was called *Eagle Head*. He lived a few doors down from *Freddie Pinhead.*

Marble Head, *Mallet Head*, *Frankie Head* – They were all stubborn, hard headed, in phonetic Italian, Gabbados.

You could see *Frankie Head* in the Wanderers, dancing in the last scene of the movie.

Egghead: His head was shaped like an egg, and it also fit because he was smart too. Another guy who I graduated from grammar school with and is still a dear friend till today.

Eggplant: Because the back of his head was flat, like an eggplant. Yet another old friend who just recently passed away.

Moonshine: He was my parents' age, lived around the corner from me and it was said that the moon shined off his head because he was bald. One of his daughters was also called *Moonshine*, not because she was bald, but we all decided she needed a nickname and she got the same one as her father. His other daughter was called *Hug-A-Bones* because she was so skinny.

Anthony Tilt: His head was always tilted to one side and I think it was to his left. One time my friend *Sal Tunnel Tooth* (who fucked with everyone!) tried to straighten *Anthony Tilt's* head because we were afraid he was going to tilt all the way over and fall, but his head always went back to that tilt.

Chickenhead and Chickenhead Jr. – They were brothers who hung out in 3rd Street Park. They both combed their hair back into a D.A. (a duck's ass) with a pompadour on top, that flopped in front of their eyes. On a chicken, it's called an "upright comb," that is this blade of flesh from the top to the back on the chicken's head, pointing straight up, and these brothers kind of looked like those chickens. I believe *Chickenhead* is *Pregnant Head's* brother-in-law – I guess these Heads gotta stick together!

Don't Have A Hairy!

Hairy Canary: Do you really need to ask? This guy lived up the street from me and was "one of the guys."

Jerry Kinks: He had fuzzy hair. He was an excellent trumpet player and even played at Carnegie Hall at some point. He was a dear friend who I haven't seen in many years, and I hope he's doing well.

Fuzzy: My cousin who had kinky hair.

Richie Bleach, a.k.a. _Richie Blood_: Richie crosses categories but was known as _Bleach_ because he was known to bleach his hair quite a bit. And Blood because he got hurt a lot while high on barbiturates. Another unfortunate casualty of the drug culture.

Noodlehead: My wife was called that as a kid because her head was covered with blonde curls like egg noodles, while everyone else in her family had dark, brown hair. When we moved to our current neighborhood, our friend's daughter had almost the same head of hair, so to us, she also became _Noodlehead._

Ringing In The Ears

As my brother so eloquently put it about anyone with big ears, "He's got some set of doors!"

Flub-A-Dub: He lived down the street from me and we hung out on the bridge over the Gowanus Canal, and… he had big ears.

Jerry Ears: As indicated with the nickname, his ears were also big. For one of the Christmas holidays when I was about 19 or 20 years old, I spent an entire week at his house after a really great Christmas party. He came from a good family, really good people.

Tin-Ear: This guy couldn't hear too well. He was one of my father's friends.

And then there was _Nee Fee_; he had one ear. When we were kids, our parents would tell us if we didn't clean our ears that potatoes would grow in them, then a bug would come eat the potatoes and our ears, just like _Nee Fee_. That was motivation to scrub our ears till no end. The rest of our body could have been filthy-dirty, but our ears sparkled!

The Eyes Have It

Popeye: There were two of them. One was the other of the bartenders at my first wedding, and I think he got his nickname because his eyes looked like they were popping out of his head. For some years, he lived in the same building as my late mother-in-law.

The other *Popeye* was the brother of *Richie Mel*, *Jimmy Psycho*, *Juju* the seven-fingered thief and their sister Carol. I don't know if this *Popeye* was called *Popeye* because his eyes bulged or because he liked the Popeye cartoon. Whatever the reason for his nickname, I'm putting him here.

Magoo: Another guy named Louie. He had bad vision and because of it, was nicknamed for Mr. Magoo who was a cartoon character with really bad vision.

Stevie-Eyeballs: This is one of those that I don't know how he got the name, but I've known the man for sixty years by that name. A few years ago, when I was on Court Street, *Eyeballs* was standing on a corner with a really small dog. I walked up to him and said, "You got some face for a little dog like that!" *Stevie-Eyeballs* said back to me, "Hey Lenny, don't break balls. I just had a fight with my wife and I'm waiting for someone to say something to me about this dog, so I can kick the shit out of them." I put my hands up at chest-level, in a push-away position and said to him, "Don't start with me!"

Marble-Eyes, *Bugg-Eyes* and *Freddie the Frog*: Why? Because they all had big eyes, A.K.A., they look like they're permanently strangled... as if someone has their hands wrapped around their troats (Brooklynese for throat), and their eyes are about to pop out of their heads. Unlike some of the Heads, none of these guys married into any other 'eyeball' families, as far as I know...

Cockeyed Mike: This is the only thing I know about this guy and that he couldn't see too well. A description of his eyes was, one eye was looking at you, and the other eye is chasing squirrels (how's that Rick?), just like my friend *Babes*, who we'll talk more about later.

Donald and Richie Cha-God: Two guys who were brothers and they were from the neighborhood. We called them *Cha-God* because they couldn't see too well. So, Donald told my wife that I surround myself with really crazy people, so no one knows how nuts I really am! Was that nice??

Who Nose

Jimmy Football Nose and *Rubber-Nose Willie*: Two more guys from the neighborhood and like our friend Lucille used to say about my friend *C.P.* and me, "their noses turned the corner before they did." You can put these two guys in the same camp as us.

Frankie Smash: Another one of my father's friends, and his nose was flat. I don't think he earned that nose as a fighter, I think it was a gift from Mother Nature.

Twitch: Josephine (my friend Nunzi's sister). We called her *Twitch* because she twitched her nose just like Elizabeth Montgomery in Bewitched did, but on queue for us when we asked her.

Lips, Lips And More Lips

Anthony Lips and *Johnny Lips*: Two more guys who happen to be brothers, so I guess you could say they were the *Lips* brothers who had big lips run in their family.

Anthony Lips and *Philly Horseteeth* used to have some rackets together, doing what they knew how to do to make a living. They'd go to junkyards to get the registration and VIN plate from the dashboard of a junked foreign sports car. Then, they would steal a similar car, replace the VIN plate with the one from the junkyard car, paint the stolen car a new color and sell it to someone for $500 to $1,000, which was a bunch of money back at the end of the 1960s. They sold one of those cars to one of my cousins, and it got stolen. The police brought the car back to my cousin because that's how good *Anthony Lips* and *Philly Horseteeth* were at this "scene," which is what we called that whole process of what they did. And by the way, they never got caught, but you could never do that today!

You're An Ass-Man!

Anthony Lard-Ass: He was from Red Hook, I guess this was his nickname because he had a big ass. He is the cousin of one of our married-in relations.

Bubble-Ass: Because he had a big ass, another guy I only knew of.

Half-Ass: Because he had a small ass. He was a kid I grew up with, and for no other reason but that we were kids, we had to fight each other every day, just for shits and giggles. Unfortunately, he died in Vietnam.

Goolahstort: In proper Italian, it would be "culo storto," which means crooked ass. My father gave that name to my cousin and every time we spoke about him, that's what we called him: *Goolahstort*, the Brooklynized version of the term. This is the man who taught me what it meant to be on time. There's much more about him in the "STORIES" chapter.

It Wouldn't Be Brooklyn Without Guys Being Known For Their "Private Parts"

Sal the Horse: Known to be well endowed, or wasn't it obvious just by the name? Our families know each other for generations.

Joe Dick: Don't ask me anything else about him, aside from him being from Brooklyn, this is all I know.

Dada: Was a guy in the neighborhood. Another one that I have no other information about because I never hung out with him, I just knew of him.

Anthony One Ball: my sister and my wife keep asking, why or how would anyone know this?! He lived down the street from me in Brooklyn and was also known as *Anthony Penguin*, not sure why.

Michael Beesche, *Sally Beesche* and *Benny Beesche* – Beesche is Italian-American slang for a man's genitalia. I don't know if any of them were given the *Beesche* moniker for being well-endowed, for being 'ladies men' or for some disfiguration, I only know this was what they were called. By the way, the *Beesches* are not related, but they each lived on a block within a three-block run: Carroll, President and Union Streets.

Legs And Feets, Don't Fail Me Now!

Louie Legs (a.k.a., *Louie Diamonds*): I was with Louie as a little kid at Bay 14 on Coney Island Beach, where Louie and some other guy bumped into each other. Louie said, "Excuse me." The other guy's response to Louie was, "Watch where the fuck you're going!" In the blink of an eye, Louie who was a lefty, clocks the guy and the guy winds up flat on his back on the sand. Without missing a beat, Louie turns to me and *Scooter* and says, "Come on, I'll take yous for some ice cream." I spoke to my friend Scooter the other day and he told me the same exact story, and that's when I realized that he was there too. I didn't remember this until I spoke with *Scooter*.

I have a thing about lefties because my father was left-handed. When I was growing up, I didn't understand that anyone could use their left hand the way I use my right hand; it just didn't register. And the pain in the ass that I was, I was always fooling around at the dinner table which was a huge 'no-no' in an Italian household. When I found myself sitting on my father's left-side, I couldn't get away fast enough from that quick left when he'd use it to slap me, to stop me from screwing around. It took a few good slaps before it penetrated that he was left-handed and what that meant for me when I was doing something wrong. I finally wised up and moved to the other side of the table and out of his reach.

Legs Ride Again!

Rider: Like me, he's bowlegged but more pronounced, so it looked to us like he just got off a horse. One day I called on Rider to go to the beach. As he was leaving his house, his mother called after him and yelled, "Michael, if you drown, don't come home!" I asked him, "Is she kidding?" He said back to me, "Don't mind her." He's still a dear friend.

Louie Short Legs: This should speak for itself and this is all I know about him.

Billy Duck Feet: Because he walked like a duck. This guy was a little older than me and came from Fourth Aven and DeGraw.

Known For Getting Hurt, Or An Injury, Or A Health Condition, *Nothing's Sacred*

Bobby Bumps: There were two of them. One was from Third Aven and the other from DeGraw Street (see earlier in this chapter).

Peels: He peeled a scab off his face once, and that was it. Peels and I went to grammar school together and we had a lot of things in common, but the most important is that we had the same family structure, kid-wise: I went to school with Peels, his younger brother went to school with my younger brother, and our younger sisters went to school together too. I basically know him for about 60 years and he never changed from then till now.

So while _Peels_ and I were in class one day, Sister Mary Richard asked Peels to multiply, and he replied, "What do you mean my mother is blind??" So, he got the shit kicked out of him by the nun. Then he told her, "I'm going to get my father after you!" The nun hit him harder. Another time Peels came into school looking like Louie Armstrong because he had a circle burned into his lips, which looked to me like he was playing the trumpet non-stop for a week. When I asked him what happened, he said that someone wanted to know if the cigarette lighter in the car worked, so he kissed it...

Linda Fits: We went to high school together. As I think back, she must have had epilepsy and of course back then, we didn't understand, so we called her _Linda Fits_, and we said that she "took fits." I guess you'd call it a colloquial term of its time, which would lead my wife to ask me, "Where was Linda taking those fits to?" Did I say that my wife likes to break my balls?

Joey Peg-Leg: Because he broke his leg and he walked with a limp like Peter Stuyvesant. For those interested in learning about the reference, Peter Stuyvesant was a 17th Century Director of New Netherlands which is probably the equivalent of a governor. Stuyvesant High School, Bed-Stuy and Stuy-Town were all named for him – and he lost the lower part of his leg due to a Spanish cannonball, resulting in his having a wooden or pegged leg.

Hands Full Of Fingers

JuJu or _JuJu Mariool_: The seven-fingered thief, who, while he was robbing copper off one of those huge wooden spools owned by the electric company, lost three fingers because it rolled over them, crushing them and requiring amputation. Despite losing his fingers, he was still a good thief. His brothers were _Richie Mel_, _Jimmy Psycho_, _Lullaby_ or _Alibi_, and _Popeye._ They also had a sister named Carol. I saw _JuJu_ dig holes for the foundation of South Brooklyn Caskett on President St. between Third Aven and Nevins Street with just a hand shovel. When he got thirsty, we used to get him a bottle of Tab (who remembers Tab, one of the first diet colas?), from Otto's candy store.

Frankie Crab-claws: He is _Jerry Ears'_ brother and a little younger than me. Frankie has big hands, which must have helped him play football because he was a good football player.

People By How They Look

Frankie Tonto: He reminded people of Jay Silverheels who played the role of Tonto in the Lone Ranger TV show.

Skins: I don't know why he was called Skins or even his real first name, but he married my cousin. I'm putting him in this category because I'm guessing this is a good place to be.

Jerry Shades and _Joey Shades_, _Hollywood Angelo_ – All three of these guys wore sunglasses all the time, but I also saw them without.

Goobie: is another sunglasses guy, but with him, for as long as I knew him, I never saw him without dark sunglasses, ever. He lived across the street from _Bobbie Bagels_ at the end of Henry Street. AND, I found out just recently what his real name was; William G. _Goobie_ and a bunch of other guys (_Sickness_, _Dennis Porter, Tu-Tu_, _Jackie African_, _Sims_, _Jimmy G._ and _Tommy Zack_), used to cop drugs from the Sullivan Hotel in the Hook during the 1960s. All of those guys except _Sickness_ and maybe _Tu-Tu_, are dead now, casualties of the drug culture. I'm told _Jackie African_ was killed trying to defend an elderly woman who was being robbed.

Eddie Chink, _Sally Chink_ and _Joanne Chink_: None are related to each other, but _Joanne Chink_ was my cousin, her brother was my cousin Georgie of the _Who Me?_ gang fame, and her sister is _Mary Apples_. _Eddie Chink_ was from Fifth Aven, _Sally Chink_ was from Red Hook. Remember, I didn't give these names or most others, I'm just telling you who had what nickname.

Emil the Duck: This guy looked like a duck and spoke like Daffy Duck.

Casper, As in "The Friendly Ghost" because he was so light, that he was white as a ghost. He is the grandson of _Goolahstort_. How many of you remember the cartoon Casper the Friendly Ghost? Or its theme song?

Color-ing Wayyyy Outside The Lines!

There were three guys called _Whitey_, one because he looked like a California surfer boy with platinum blonde hair and a tan year-round. He had an easy-going strut about him. During the summer, he strolled the bays of Coney Island Beach in Brooklyn, always by himself, looking good and drinking beer. Unfortunately, he became badly addicted to drugs is no longer among the living.

My cousin Tony Cat was a fireman for 42 years, and they called him _Whitey_, also because he was really blonde. A few years ago, right after Tony died, I visited the firehouse where he worked and I got really choked up when they showed me that they kept his chair with his name on it, and because he did so much in support of his firefighter brothers and sisters, no one is allowed to sit in Tony's chair. After he retired from the FDNY, every second Wednesday of the month, Tony cooked for the "On the Arm" free breakfasts. He took part in other volunteer efforts in support of Friends of Firefighters as well. He's been called "a fireman's fireman."

Then there was another really blonde guy from Red Hook who was one more _Whitey_, but some years back, when he was really high on drugs, he killed his mother... Unlike the first _Whitey_, there were no easy-going -surfer-dude personality traits for this guy being called _Whitey_. Anyway, in the early 2000s, this _Whitey_ was finally released from prison and was at a Bar-B-Q I went to with my wife and infant daughter. As _Whitey_ and I were catching up about the goings on in the old neighborhood, I took my daughter and put her in his arms as my wife, clutched my hand and looked on, horrified. She wanted to kill me! She said that she fought really hard to keep her composure so as not upset _Whitey_ with her reaction to him, so he wouldn't take it out in some sick way on the baby. I told her, "The baby was never in any danger because I was right there, but he might of taken it out on you!"

Blackie: He was one of only a few Black people in our neighborhood, so that's what we called him and one of the guys whose real name remains unknown to me, _Blackie_. _Blackie_ was one tough guy! When we were all in the Lil' Gents, he and Louie G. had a fight for a good fifteen minutes on Fourth Aven between Sackett and DeGraw Streets. Neither one of them gave up, but they stopped after 15 minutes and called it even.

Black Betty: The first woman I ever had sex with, which cost me a dollar in 1962 when I was 11. I always say that I had a tickle in my ass and it felt good. Betty was a woman trying to make a living, but in today's world, she would be considered a pedophile even though I initiated the situation.

Rosie Black: Her hair was deep black.

Greenie: A guy I grew up with, but I think his real name was Anthony (of course

108

we called him Antnee). *Greenie* and I used to deliver newspapers together. He had the thickest eyebrows we ever saw, and an even bigger smile.

Red and *Eddie Red* and *Louie Red/Bonzo* – all three because they had red hair. I was in *Eddie Red's* bridal party when he got married. *Louie Red/Bonzo* lived on Whitwell Place. He got the name *Bonzo* because he was big.

Guys Known For An Ethnicity, Not Necessarily Their Own

Jackie the African: He was a white guy who was born in Africa (not sure where) and was part of the *Sinclair's*. This guy would pull a knife on anyone to rob them. But in a twist of fate, when he was in his thirties, I heard he was in Florida and ran to the aid of an elderly woman who was being robbed at knifepoint. To defend this woman, he pulled a knife on the would-be robbers, but they killed him with their knives. I guess you can see that he both lived and died by the knife, but dying as a hero.

Johnny the Greek: I think he lived next door to *Butchie Black*, and we think he got his name was because he was Greek. He drove limousines with my dad.

Frankie the Zip or *Frankie the WOP*: Italian, period. Nothing more to offer about this guy. This is an instance of an epithet being embraced by those it was hurled at.

(Sally) The Geep: Calling him *The Geep* is because that's another slang term for an Italian. When my cousin Donny M. tells me that he spoke to *The Geep*, that's all he has to say because I know exactly who he means. Both my cousin and *The Geep* were tough football players.

John Australian: Because he was born in Australia. He was part of the *Sinclair's* and whenever he greeted someone, instead of saying, "Hi," he would say, "Aye."

Murphy: A guy who looked Irish but was actually Italian. According to my brother, he was also known as *Pigeon Shit*. Then there were his other nicknames of *Surf Bruce* and *Sea Dog*. His father was called *Jellybeans*. One of his brothers was Nibsy and the other was called *Joe Bo*. I knew him from when I was two years old and he's another of my friends who are no longer with us. He too is a casualty of the drug culture.

Stevie The Russian: His wife Ruthie looked and spoke like Edward G. Robinson (I can't imagine how this match could work!). He was about 5 foot 7, and really thick, but one tough guy. I *think* he might have been Russian.

Puerto Rican Louie: He was good friends with my cousin Tommy W. By the way, both were non Italians, but since they were related to Italians, it made them acceptable in our neighborhood. *Puerto Rican Louie* was actually Puerto Rican, and he always had a big smile on his face.

Guys (and Girls) Because of Their Size (Like I Said, *Nothing's Sacred*)

Doll-Doll: I'm not sure why she was called *Doll-Doll*, but I'm putting her here because it's the likeliest place. She used to hang out with us in the candy store. She was very pretty, but what you might call chubby back then – today, she'd probably be normal weight!

Big Sal, *Sally Buff*, *Big Jackie*, *Frankie The Animal*, *Anthony The Beast* and *Big Ralph* – because they're all big. *Big Sal* and *Sally Buff* hung out with us when we stayed on Fifth Aven. *Big Jackie* and I graduated from grammar school together, and whenever we took a picture, we were always next to each other.

Anthony Hercules: Was a small guy who was NOT Hercules; he was really skinny. Anthony was a friend of mine, but was closer with my brother. He was a great guy, an EMT who unfortunately died on the Belt Parkway when someone cut him off causing his Corvette to bash into the guardrail and explode in flames. His colleagues couldn't get to him in time... What a terrible loss!!

Midget: He was small. I'm sorry if this upsets anyone... His real name was Michael, but no one knew him as Michael. Again, someone from my neighborhood marrying someone else from my neighborhood, he married my cousin Emily. Another good softball player.

Pee-Wee: A guy who lived in the house we later bought and he hung out in one of the social clubs.

Shorty: This is what we called my uncle Joe, who was short and worked at the Coca-Cola bottling plant that was down the block from us. He used to call me "The Wandering Kid."

We also called a girl from Court Street *Shorty* and to this day, I have no idea what her real name is, but I do know that she married one of the "*Reds*."

Mousie: she was a pretty girl and really small. Her brother was Pregnant Head. She and her family lived directly across the street from our parish.

Fat Allie: Why? Because he was fat. _Fat Allie_ asked my wife when he met her, if she had sneakers. He told her to put them on and "RUN!" We loved _Fat Allie_, and just about everyone else we mention in this book, but he died in the early 2000s at the Applebee's in Sheepshead Bay. We were told that he died the way he lived. He had a massive heart attack and died with a cheeseburger in one hand and a broad in the other. Naturally, he was no longer _Fat Allie_; he became _Allie Applebee_.

Buffalo: One more fat guy and very nice – we'd say that he was a "piece of bread." Unfortunately he lost his eye when he got hit square in that eye by a Roman Candle on July 4th one year.

Fat Ernie: He was a little older than me and known for having banged _Black Betty_ (_Black Betty_ was the local hooker and was an African American woman), in the back of Farmer Jones' station wagon, according to _Vinny The Boob_. _Fat Ernie_ is a guy who was always into mischief. He was a schemer and you could see it because even when he was talking to and looking at you, you could see the wheels were turning in his head. His uncle was _Honey_.

Fat Rosie: Another of my mother's friends who lived up the block from us. She had an awning on the front of her house with her name on it. She once asked my son Joseph, "Do you like peaches? Then take a bite of my ass!" Everyone was a character in our neighborhood!

Tiny: Today he would shop in the big and tall store; he was about 6' 4" and about 300 lbs. _Tiny_ had two brothers, Joe and Bobby who were almost as big, but _Tiny_ dominated them by beating them up daily. His routine was to alternate which brother to throw a beating on; one brother one day, and then the other brother got it the next day. So at one point, Bobby and Joe decided to gang up on _Tiny_ when he was asleep, because that was their best chance. Bobby and Joe entered the room and had nothing to hit _Tiny_ with but a crucifix from the wall (if anyone remembers, in a Catholic household, there was always a crucifix over the kids' beds in those days). So they pulled the crucifix off the bedroom wall and proceeded to try to beat the piss out of _Tiny_. Well, _Tiny_ started to get off the bed, that's when Bobby and Joe threw the crucifix at him and ran away because they saw that _Tiny_ was barely flinching. It was like shooting b-b's at an elephant, he wasn't phased in the least, just irritated.

Baby Huey: Like many of the people I mention, he was a happy-go-lucky kid, and we got sodas from his grandfather's candy store on Fifth Aven, on the way to play softball. He got this nickname because he was shaped like the Donald Duck cartoon character. If you ever saw any of the Donald Duck cartoons with Baby Huey, he was an adult duck in a diaper with a safety pin holding it together, wearing a baby bonnet tied under his chin and a tiny blue shirt.

Butterball: Another heavy guy who was a pretty good softball player and I think he was from Court Street. I also had a cousin who we called _Butterball_.

Anthony Moose: He's about 6'2" and 260 lbs. I'm not sure how he makes this connection, but any time anyone wanted to have Chinese food, he'd refuse and say that it was because the Japanese bombed Pearl Harbor! For a few years he worked at a Pizzeria on Court and DeGraw Streets, and when he asked the owner for a raise, his boss said 'no,' so Anthony quit. The owner of that pizzeria realized he made a big mistake when it took two guys to replace Anthony, so he asked Anthony to come back. This was the same scenario that happened when my Aunt Dora asked for a raise, was refused and quit; her bosses had her come back when it took two people to do her job too.

The (Da) Ox: This guy was big and **_really_** strong.

On President Street, between Third Aven and Nevins Street was a Coca-Cola bottling plant where all us kids would wander into to see if there were any loose 6 oz bottles of soda to rob. When I was about 10 or 11 years old, _Richie Mel_ and I got onto the roof of the factory from the President Street side of the building. We ran up the back stairwell of the plant up to the roof where we played and were oblivious about the time of day because kids didn't wear watches back then, the only time that mattered was what time we were supposed to be home for dinner. So without a watch, we didn't realize it was past 5 o'clock which meant it was after workers in the plant closed the roof door and went home, meaning no one knew we were up there. With the building being empty and no access to any staircases, we had to figure out on our own how to get down from the roof, so we looked around and found a rope up there that we tied to a smokestack so we could try repelling down on the Nevins Street side of the building and stay out of sight. Richie went first but the rope broke and he fell a few feet, landing in an empty lot below, across from another empty lot and Akers Trucking Company that was also closed because it was after working hours; thankfully Richie wasn't hurt. He stood up, brushed off his butt, then looked up at me and I told him to go around the corner onto President Street to the candy store where a bunch of the guys from the neighborhood were hanging out, to see if any of them could help me get down. Someone at the candy store went and got _The Ox,_ and once he saw me on the roof, the only thing he said was for me to jump, that he'd catch me. It was about a fifteen-foot drop without that rope, so I did what he told me to do... and he caught me, a man of his word! Looking back, this may have been another early step prepping me for stunt work.

Power House: John M. was another strong guy, he was also a great softball player who was a little older than us. Whenever we had money games against another neighborhood, everyone always asked _Power House_ to play on our team.

Eddie Pole: Because he was as skinny as a pole. My wife started cracking up when I mentioned Eddie; she's very visual and said it was because she imagined him to be some 15-foot pole with nothing but eyes and eyebrows somewhere high up on it, like Mr. Potato Head.

Pickles: He was skinny too and was a little older than me. _Pickles_ introduced us all to the Police Athletic League (the P.A.L.). Each precinct sponsored a youth team to play baseball, and our rivalry was against the 76th pct because we played for the 7-8.

Tommy Zach: He too, was really skinny and looked like John Zacherly, a really scary guy from the horror shows on TV in the 50s and 60s. He was my dear friend, but unfortunately he died from A.I.D.S. some time ago. When I lived next door to Monte's restaurant, I ran into Tommy's nephew who said, my uncle always spoke highly of you, which was an honor.

These Last Ones, Because They Deserve Their Own Section

Muscles... because he had none. He lived up the block from my paternal grandparents and some other people we knew. His brother was _Lenny Mutt_ who made sounds like a dog, for no reason, he'd just yelp or bark like a dog.

Philly Horseteeth... because he did! By the way, you can read more about Philly with _Anthony Lips_.

Well, strange as it may seem, all of these nicknames are true. This is Brooklyn at its best.

TRADITIONS:

KNOWING THE DAYS OF THE WEEK BY THE FOOD WE ATE

Most of the many traditions we Italians had have been about food, and the time we ate was a big part of this. You had to be home and ready to eat at 5 o'clock p.m. when food was on the table on a weekday, or there would be hell to pay. The foods we ate depended on the day of the week and it was so consistent that I could of been deprived of light or access to a calendar, gone without one person speaking to me... but I knew what day of the week it was because of what we were eating. Saturdays meant it was steak night, and everyone in the whole apartment building used the 'apartment house BBQ': *steak cooked directly on the stove's grating*, right over the gas burner flame, which made so much smoke that it poured out into the hallways so much that you could barely see your hand in front of your face, and being inside of any one of the apartments in the building was just as worse! It was almost like the Great Chicago Fire or a really foggy London day – because everyone in the building was doing it at the same time, the exact same way. But let me tell you, it did smell amazing! If you ever cooked on one of these grates like that, then you know what I mean. Also, we used that same apartment house BBQ to fire-roast peppers. My grandmother used to put the peppers directly on top of the fire until the skin was a burnt crust that she peeled off. She added oil, spice and walla (voilà), we had roasted peppers.

Sunday, Oh Sunday! Fugettaboutit!! We would all gather at my grandparents' apartment and honestly, it was a banquet, a marathon day of cooking and eating. My grandmother (my mom's mom) started cooking at 8 o'clock Sunday morning, usually with my mother helping. All us kids went to church; the kitchen was church for the women. Two o'clock is when we started eating and everyone **HAD** to be there, no excuses. Family and food were what was important, and unless they had their own Italian Sunday dinner with mandatory attendance, sometimes we had friends over too because there was ALWAYS more than enough food. We would start off with macaroni, then we went to the meats: sausage, spareribs, brachiola, pieces of pork, pork skin, meatballs and my personal favorite, pork neckbones which gave the gravy (sauce to other people) flavor. OMG! I can smell it right now as I'm writing this. On certain occasions we had a treat like homemade raviolis or homemade monegotts (manie-cotti to the non-Brooklyn Eye-Talians!). My grandmother had to lay them out on the bed on a clean white sheet, because it was the only place in the apartment that could hold all of those monegotts and raviolis at the same time. I used to help my grandmother crush the tomatoes by hand into a colander with a bowl under it. Despite how we tried not to waste anything, the only exception was the seeds from crushing the tomatoes because they made the gravy bitter. Some people included the seeds and either threw in a little sugar to sweeten it or baking soda to cut the acidity of the gravy.

After the macaroni and meat gravy, we'd take a little time to digest, maybe an hour or two. All the kids would sing and dance while my grandfather played the castanets. The men did not do a thing! They left everything to the women to take care of; from cooking, cleaning the table, and setting the table for the next course, which was chicken with some sort of salad or andhe-bahst (anti-pasta), that never left the table until it was completely done. My father made a meal out of the andhe-bahst – black olives, anchovies (aleege), artichoke hearts, tomatoes, prosciutto, sopressata, regular boiled ham, mozzarella, brovahlone (provolone to the uninitiated), vinegar peppers, stuffed mushroom caps and a little Italian bread with olive oil and vinegar – different people did it their own way, adding other things to their smorgasbord.

Till this day, I don't know how we got that many people into that little 4 room apartment. But then again, we figured it all out - the little kids might sit in the hall, on the hard marble steps, and, of course, running the hall or up and down the stairs in between bites of food. The older adults took their seats at the table, with the younger adults or older kids sitting in the living room or on my cousin's bed that was in the next room. It didn't matter as long as everyone ate and stayed together because that was the point. And, by the way, that apartment is still occupied by my Aunt Josie and has been occupied by some part of my family since at least the early 1950s.

Last, but certainly not least was dessert with brown and black coffee (the latter also known as Italian amphetamines). By this point, it's 8 pm and half of the day (as in 12 hours) was gone. A day that consisted of preparing, cooking and eating, and eating ... and eating. The easiest part was going home because we all lived in the same apartment building. This was heaven!

The same ritual happened on Saturdays at my paternal grandparents' house on DeGraw Street, which was another Holy Grail. But for some reason (...I was told ... that I was too much to watch – you know, I should be scarred by this!), my grandparents wouldn't let me upstairs! A couple of years ago, I was standing outside of that house and the current owner asked me if he could help me. I told him that I have a lot of history in that house and when he realized that he bought it from my Aunt Dolly and my Uncle Johnny, he asked me to come in. When this nice man, who didn't know me from Adam, offered to let me go upstairs to see the second floor, I told him, "No! No! No! I wasn't allowed up there when I was a kid, I'm not going up there now!" My wife laughs at me that I'm still irked by this. Oh, and by the way, that house on DeGraw Street is where my friend Andrew Gimme Room was born.

Here's What Italian Mothers And Grandmothers Were, And In Some Homes Today, Still Are, And How They Ran The House:

1. She sits down to eat only when everyone else is already seated.

2. She always has containers or plastic storage bags for her guests to fill with leftovers to take home – there's always leftovers because she cooks for a friggin army.

3. No one can be trusted alone in her kitchen.

4. When someone comes over, the first thing the woman of the house wants to do is feed them. The man however, will ask you what you want to drink. (Remember this Ray?)

5. She thinks there's a major problem, that maybe you're dead in some ditch somewhere if you don't immediately answer her calls.

6. Her children are very protective of her. Here's a 'for instance': I happened to call my mother up (this was after my father passed away, the old Italians never remarried), and she told me there was a friend that she had at the house with her - a man. I forget where I was, but because my brother wasn't home, I started calling all my cousins up, saying that my mother was home with a strange man. When I finally got to our apartment, there was about five of my cousins there; my mother introduced me to the "strange man," and he seemed like a nice guy, but he told my mother that we were very overprotective of her. Turns out the "strange man" was an old friend of my mother's, but me, being the traditionalist that I am, I couldn't see my mother with any man but my father, even though he was dead.

7. When old Italian women became widows, they wore black for the rest of their lives to mourn their husbands, like many Mediterranean and traditional cultures.

8. It may seem odd now since fedora hats aren't really worn anymore, but NO HATS ON THE TABLE! This was a superstition about it being bad luck to put your hat on a table. Well, it really came from an old

belief that hats, *and helmets,* had germs, so the women didn't want anyone getting sick from some dirty hat laying on the table where everyone eats. Look at any films or pictures of a Brooklyn Dodger baseball game; just about every man at a game was wearing a hat, so this was for real for us. In those days, when a man walked into someone's house, he was polite and took his hat off when he came in the door, but he did not place it on the table. It was uncommon to see a man not wearing a hat back then. I also know people who don't want shoes, even brand new, never worn ones on a table or chair. Then, there are those who think it's bad luck to put a woman's pocketbook on the floor, that it means she'll always be broke. Well, if you think about both of those for a minute, you can see the germ thing maybe being the root of them too.

9.   Take it or leave it; what your mother put in front of you to eat was what was on the menu. If you didn't want to eat what was on the plate, you went hungry. But let's get real, this was more of the father's rule than anyone's mother's because if mom thought you weren't eating right or enough, she would twist herself into a pretzel to get you to eat something, anything, even if it was what she thought was an abnormal eating preference. Every Italian mother's ultimate goal was to get everyone, especially the kids and her husband to eat as much as possible.

10.   The salad came after dinner *or before*. Basically, it was always on the table.

11.   No business talk at the dinner table – if you saw The Godfather, this was said in one of the scenes with Sonny.

12.   Dairy, specifically cheese, does not go with fish, a big no-no! For example, if you had crabs and macaroni, there was no cheese on the table to go on the macaroni, that would be sacrilege.

13.   Don't be a gavone! Wait until all desserts are on the table before you pick what you want, and especially before you start eating your dessert.

14.   Mostly all meals are eaten with Italian bread – the end, a.k.a., **the ass** of the bread is always the best.

15.   If the phone rang during dinner, no one was allowed to answer it, and your friends weren't allowed to ring the bell during dinner time, it was a cardinal sin! All us kids knew what time dinner was at each

other's houses, so we all knew not to interrupt anyone else's dinner. Try that today, with everyone's smartphones as appendages; good luck!

16. A tradition in our house was when we had creamed corn or niblet corn from a can, my mother had to serve it in a coffee cup. I have no idea how this started, but that was the way we ate it. My brother's ex-father-in-law was having dinner with us and when he saw my mother put the coffee cups on the table, he asked if we were having coffee early – when she told him it was for the corn, he told her, "You really spoil them." She brushed it off by saying, "Ah, you know how it is." My mother liked to indulge us, so her menu was a little more flexible than some other Italian mothers and grandmothers. She used two different store-bought breadcrumbs to make chicken cutlets because my brother and I liked different kinds, as well as different types of Italian bread and regular, sliced bread.

More Traditions And Neighborhood-Specific Odd Ball Things, Some Just In Our House

1. If milk was used in coffee, you couldn't drink *that* milk from a glass, because it was reserved only for coffee and then it became "coffee milk." (Right C.P. and Pete?)

2. When a woman was pregnant, a pool was organized to see who could guess the baby's weight. Whoever had the closest guess would win all of the money. Gambling was big in my neighborhood. I knew people who would bet on running water!

3. When a woman gave birth to a baby, the father gave out cigars, which probably doesn't happen anymore.

4. Another tradition around a new addition to a family was to name the new baby after its grandparents, the father's parents first. Like in my family, me being the first-born boy, I was named for my father's father, and my sister as the first and only girl, was named for my father's mother. I've carried on with this tradition by naming my son and daughter for my parents too. My wife can tell you, that if she wouldn't of agreed to do this, we wouldn't be married (at this point, she might be rethinking that!!).

5. The Italian version of Alka-Seltzer was Brioschi that we took for stomach pains, also known as ah-gih-dah. I know a few people who are good at giving ah-gih-dah!

6. When someone had a pimple, they would use toothpaste or Noxzema to draw it out.

7. Pastina was eaten when someone had a cold, with butter and/or milk and no matter how soupy we tried to make it, whatever juice it was in always got soaked up to make it thick and gloppy. If any of you remember when your mom wanted to get you to eat something, she might tell you to open the door or open the airplane hangar! My mom told me to open the airplane hangar as she gave me a nice big spoon full of pastina, and right after it was in my mouth, I'd blow pastina raspberries all over her and whatever she was wearing!

8. Italian penicillin: garlic and pastina, not necessarily together.

9. Italian steroids: pasta fazool – macaroni and beans.

10. The Grand Poo-Pah of cold remedies was Vick's VapoRub. First, you rub it on your chest or under your nose when you were congested. And if you wanted to get it deeper into your sinus membranes, you mixed a spoonful of Vick's VapoRub into boiling water, with a towel big enough to go over your head and around the sides of the pot so you could inhale it. When I was a kid and I had a sore throat, I decided since Vick's VapoRub helped with congestion, it would be just as good for a sore throat... so I ate it ...and I felt it worked! My cousin Carmela would agree with me that eating Vicks helped when we were sick. My wife thinks that explains a few things about me. One of my swimmers, Morgan, a few years ago said, "That says a lot, Lenny!" And Ms. Fitpatrick agrees. Ok, I don't know that I should recommend anyone else eat Vick's, so kids, DON'T TRY THIS AT HOME!! Maybe they're right: It tells you a little about us!

11. When any of us kids were sick, my Aunt Anna was the one who took care of us with alcohol sponge baths to help bring down the fever. There was something about when my Aunt Anna did this that was special, it made us feel a whole lot better.

12. For teething babies or if someone had a toothache, you'd rub whiskey on the gums. I don't know if the baby's gums were soothed or they were pacified by the alcohol!

13.   And who remembers how diapers were cleaned before there was such things as disposable diapers? You took the diaper off the child, the contents (if there were any) were emptied into the toilet, then they were usually washed separately from the rest of the laundry and I'm sure I don't need to explain why...

14.   When passing in front of a church of my own faith (Catholic), I'll make the sign of the cross. My wife says the Greeks do this too, when passing a Greek Orthodox church.

15.   Opening an umbrella in the house is bad luck. In my neighborhood, umbrellas were another weapon, so maybe opening one inside the house could be the start of a fight!

16.   Spilling milk on the table and the spill goes toward someone, it's good luck for that person. Someone said it had something to do with angels or something.

17.   Stepping in dog shit is good luck. God only knows why!

18.   A rabbit's foot is good luck. I love this! If it's such good luck, why doesn't the rabbit still have that foot??

19.   Horseshoe over the door is good luck, maybe because it looks like a magnet and will catch the good luck.

20.   For us, the trunk of an Elephant pointing up and facing the door is good luck. My wife's family believed that if it points down it's good luck. Go figure...

21.   Red Italian horn hanging from a car's rear-view mirror is supposed to keep the maloikia (bad vibes or bad luck) away.

22.   When a girl and a guy were "an item," they were going steady, and the guy would give her an ankle bracelet that she would wear on her left ankle to show that she was taken.

23.   Like I said at the opening of this chapter, I knew the day of the week by the food my mother cooked. Monday, no matter how cold or hot out, we had soup, mostly Beef soup. She'd also make us Lipton soup and sometimes added egg to it. And of course, chicken soup.

Friday was fish or pizza, never meat. Back in those days, the Catholic Church required Fridays to be meatless.

Saturday was steak. Like I said, anyone living in an apartment house might know about cooking steak on top of the burners of the stove; none of us had a gas grill. Fifteen other families in our building did the exact same thing, so the smoke that went through the apartment building was thick enough to cut with a knife.

Many years later when I lived in Kansas, I worked in a slaughterhouse and I used to pick up the scraps of meat that fell onto the fat when the cut-man cut up the beef. Sometimes, we asked him to make the cuts different so we could get some good scraps to take home and eat. One day Mark T. and I went to our friend Ichabod's house to have a Bar-B-Que with some of those scraps from the slaughterhouse – skirt steaks (they're not scraps anymore!)! I asked Ichabod if he had a grill and a rack to put steaks on, but he didn't. So Mark and I, thinking outside the box, noticed that his roommate had a parakeet in a birdcage. We opened the cage door and let the bird fly out. Then we took the cage apart and used it like a rack to cook the steaks on top of his stove with the same result as Brooklyn, lots of smoke, like the San Francisco fire but tasty as could be. The roommate came home to all the smoke and we talked him right into having some steak. He didn't notice the bird was flying around the apartment at first and that the cage was missing. When we were all done eating, we asked him how the steaks were and he said they were good. Then he asked how we cooked them and we told him what we did with the birdcage. Needless to say, he was pissed! It probably ruined his meal for him. (More about this in book 2)

Back to Sunday, like I said above, it was a day dedicated to eating.

Not Such Big Boys Toys

Our families didn't have much money and we definitely didn't have the kinds of toys then like today, so we improvised a lot by making things like our own carpet guns and scooters. We personalized what we built, which is how we showed off our personalities, and of course compare what we made with each other's – no two scooters looked the same.

We made scooters with a 2"x4" piece of wood that was about 5' long, basically making it into a skateboard with handles. For wheels, we used a pair of metal roller skates that we took apart and nailed them to one side of the 2"x4", then mounted a milk crate on the other side of that same two-by-four on what was the top side where the cab went for us to kneel behind – it was usually big enough to sit in if we nailed it in a different position. We used a wooden stick for a handle by nailing it in one piece to the top or in two pieces along the side of the wooden milk crate to steer it. And with all the bottle caps in the gutter, we nailed a bunch of them to the 2"x4" or the milk crate, painted the whole thing, then maybe take some bottle caps off to make a cool pattern. Then we kept one foot on the 2"x4" and used the other foot to push off to get the scooter rolling down the street while we steered it. You could think of these as DIY rat-rods.

In those days there was always loose wood on the street or in an empty lot. My grandfather was always good for nails and paint, and as long we could scrounge up tools and other supplies, we were kind of self-reliant. How does this stand up to what goes on today? I hate to say it, but to have a kid bang a nail and get off their computer or phone might be too risky and require unstructured imagination. I don't know, maybe it's too much work, too much imagination. How many of you agree?

A carpet gun was a glorified slingshot that we made, again, using a two-by-four piece of wood along with two nails, a wooden clothes pin and a rubber band. We put a long-ish nail at the tip of one end of the two-by-four and used a hammer to bend it over the rubber band to keep it in place, then nail the clothes pin to the other end – the nail for the clothespin had to be smaller and thinner so it didn't split the clothes pin. The rubber band needed to stretch enough to reach the clothespin without snapping or being too loose. When someone got new linoleum in their house, the old flooring was usually rolled up and left at the curb for garbage pick-up, and you could say that we were early recyclers because we helped ourselves to it... one man's junk is another man's treasure. We used cut-up pieces of one of the thrown-out linoleum as projectiles for our carpet guns (I don't know why we called it a carpet gun since there was almost never any carpeting around for us to use to shoot). And if we couldn't find any old linoleum, sometimes we used asphalt roofing or building shingles. I don't mean to sound like a crusty old man, but I really think kids today would never go to all this effort to make something so primitive like this themselves instead of buying something slick and polished in, say, the Apple store or a 3-D printer... Not only that, but I'm not sure what kid would want to go garbage-picking like we did. And in today's day and age, ripping shingles off a building would probably mean someone calling the cops on you for vandalism! Oh, the shame of it all!!

Traveling Circus/Carnies

The Whip, King Kong, a mobile Ferris-wheel, Good Humor, Mr. Softie and a pony ride showing up on our streets – this is when we knew the warm weather was coming! Likewise, we knew the bad weather was on its way when all those guys stopped coming around. The way it happened was that the rides came first in the afternoon into the early evening, then the ice cream trucks later on, just in time for dessert! This repeated just about every day from the middle of April until the middle of September, unless it was raining. When there was a block party on different streets, they'd last well into the night and these carnival rides were at one end of the block or the other. The King Kong ride was a massive seesaw or pendulum-like swing with rows of seats on two sides, that would swing so far up on each side that we hoped it would go all the way over, turning us all upside down. We all yelled for it to swing higher! The only thing holding us in our seats was centrifugal force! ... Safety? There was no thought about preventing anyone from falling out, that was part of the thrill. Then the Whip had multiple cars on a conveyer-type belt that swung us around in a circle but whipped really fast at one particular point in the ride, hence the name, the Whip. With any of the rides that came, you hoped everyone on the ride had a strong stomach and didn't just eat something that they'd wind up sharing with the other riders... And there was almost always an ice cream truck on one end of the block or the other, and like I said, if we had money left from the rides, we went and get a cone with our favorite flavor ice cream, or sundae, or an ice pop. It never failed that one of our friends would run out of money (we had to budget the quarter or 50₵ our parents gave to us for the day between calzones, ice cream and these rides), and we all knew who had extra money, so we went and grubbed (borrow) some cash from them to go on another ride or get ice cream. And if we knew that one of our friends didn't spend any or all of their own money, that's who we grubbed from. We were always looking to see when the guy running the ride was distracted so we could sneak on, because that added to the thrill of these crazy rides.

THESE ARE THE CARS FROM SOME OF THE OLD RIDES THAT WE JUST SAW HANGING FROM THE CEILING IN A STORE IN UPSTATE NEW YORK. THIS ONE WAS PROBABLY ATTACHED TO A LONG METAL ARM, LIKE A WHEEL SPOKE, THAT HAD IT ON TRACK GOING AROUND IN CIRCLES.

I'M NOT SURE ABOUT THIS ONE, BUT IT WAS PROBABLY EARTH-BOUND TOO.

THESE WERE PART OF SOME RIDES THAT CAME AROUND OR AT A KIDDIE PARK, BUT WE RODE IN THEM.

Talkin' 'Bout Our Generation

1.   A wrench, a can and a Johnny Pump (a.k.a., a fire hydrant) – that's all we needed for summer fun. This was our beach in the street. We'd open the Johnny Pump using the wrench to take off the cap on the front, usually the smaller side because we wanted the higher pressure than the larger opening, then open the valve by turning the nut on the top, almost like a faucet to make the water come gushing out. Someone would position a can over the hydrant's opening to make the water shoot through it (the can was open on both ends making it a small tube), and we directed which way the water gushed out. Back then, those cans were tin, not like the aluminum ones today, so they held up better. Sometimes, the police came by and told us to shut it down because we were wasting water and the thrust of the water pressure could make it dangerous. They'd also try to get us to use a sprinkler cap made for the larger opening of the hydrant, but we wanted all that water to come surging out, full force. When a car

came by and the driver didn't want to get hit with this rush of water, someone would sit in front of the opening to block the water, or we used our hands to push down on the stream, to aim it at the street.

2. Aside from dinner at 5:00 o'clock on weeknights and 2:00 o'clock on Sunday afternoons, we were only home to sleep (and maybe study), otherwise, we were out from the morning, until the streetlamps came on.

3. Most of us Italian kids were taught by Irish-Catholic nuns and Italian priests in Catholic grammar schools. They were long on discipline and short on compassion – read more about them in the "STORIES" chapter.

4. We collected and traded baseball cards. Little did we know how valuable they would be later on in life. If I had all the cards from back then, in decent enough condition, I could have comfortably retired 30 years ago!

5. Every kid needed permission to cross the street until our parents trusted us to do it by ourselves. The smaller streets with one-way traffic, like President Street or Carroll Street, were the first ones we were allowed to cross. The larger streets like Third Aven, had two-way traffic and so we weren't allowed to cross it for quite a while after the smaller streets.

6. We would play just about any kind of street game we could, including ball games, as long as the weather allowed. Otherwise we'd make something up.

7. Among other games, we played tag on the monkey bars in the playgrounds, but back then there were no rubber mats under them, just cement. If someone fell, it could be a bloody mess at best, or some bone broke. But if you fell, it was tough luck!

8. We sat on someone's stoop and play card games like Rummy and Brisk. More about this in the "GAMES" chapter.

9. Many of us collected empty soda bottles to get the deposit to buy candy: 2¢ for small ones, 5¢ for large bottles.

10. There were dances at our grammar school on Friday nights.

11. On Christmas Eve, everyone went to midnight mass, and then back to our own houses afterward, to eat. It was another holiday celebration

with food, a marathon of eating, and eating, and eating. And yes, we still till today have the feast of the 7 fishes to celebrate Christmas Eve. My sister is the one who hosts our family at this point and she cooks enough for an army! Thank God for her husband Rob and their kids, Britney and Robert Jr. (my godson)!

12.   Twice a year we were treated to new clothes: Easter and Christmas. No one had throw-away clothes or outfits with tags still on them hanging in their bottomless closets back then. We wore our clothes until we grew out of them or wore them out.

13.   During the summer when it was really hot, we'd use a nail to carve our names into the tar in the street. Forget about when there was new cement on the sidewalk.

14.   Boy, let me tell you, we heard the men argue hard about who was the best centerfielder in baseball – remember, we had three teams back in the early to late 50s, and they all played in NYC! Mays (NY Giants), Mantle (NY Yankees) or Snider (Brooklyn Dodgers), and no one ever came to any agreement, they just argued. Once the Dodgers and then the Giants left New York, there were broken hearts in every home! A lot of us stuck with the Dodgers, even though they went to L.A., but there were plenty more who felt betrayed and went on to root for other teams. Lots of Dodgers fans eventually went for the Mets when they had their inaugural year in 1962 and by this point, we kids carried on the tradition of doing the arguing over what players were better.

15.   When we hung out with our friends, we all met at the local candy store which was John's Candy Store, where we listened to music on the jukebox, buy 1¢ candy, 10¢ sodas, 10¢ cups of ice cream (chocolate on one side, vanilla on the other), and 5¢ pretzels. As we got older, we started hanging out in the local pool hall and eventually, the bars.

Nursery Rhymes

Clap Hands, Clap Hands – Clap hands, clap hands till daddy comes home. Daddy's got the money, and Mommy's got none.

Billy Boy, Billy Boy – Where have you been, Billy Boy, Billy Boy? Oh, where have you been, charming Billy?

I've been out to see my wife; she's the joy of my life. She's a young thing and cannot leave her mother.

Where have you been, Billy Boy, Billy Boy? Oh where have you been, charming Billy?

She can bake a cherry pie, with a twinkle in her eye. She's a young thing and cannot leave her mother.

Where have you been, Billy Boy, Billy Boy? Oh where have you been, charming Billy?

She took my hat and coat, but she gave it to a goat. She's a young thing that cannot leave her mother.

One-Two, Buckle My Shoe – I used this nursery rhyme in one of my college classes, "Public Speaking for Professionals." The topic was how we make kids learn and I used this to illustrate how to teach kids how to count. Then, I went into the Three Stooges skit about A E I O U and B A Bay, B U Bu, B I Bickie-Bie… while I was singing and dancing in front of the whole class to show how to engage students. My two friends Sully and Eddie were elbowing each other because they couldn't believe I was doing this. My professor thought it was unique, creative, and he gave me either an A or an A-. If I got an A- it was because of my singing, because I'm Italian, and all us Italians can sing! My wife thinks it was creative, unique and took balls, but then again, she's a performer and she did something similar during her undergrad.

On Top Of Old Smokey – On top of Old Smokey,

All covered with cheese,

I lost my poor meatball,

When somebody sneezed.

…*Who knows the rest of this one*?

And how about the rest of these:

1, 2, 3, Get Off My Father's Apple Tree…

Blue Bird, Blue Bird, Through My Window…

Someone and Someone Sittin In A Tree, K-I-S-S-I-N-G…

This Little Piggie…

This Old Man…

Fat and Skinny had a race…

A Tisket, A Tasket, A Brown and Yellow Basket…

Eenei, Meenie, Minie, Moe…

Yankee Doodle Went To Town…

Whistle While You Work – you can fill in the rest.

GAMES

These are the games we played. A lot of them had to do with physically hurting one another (the last person standing sort of thing). My wife said we had an uncanny way of turning the ball in just about every ballgame into a weapon. Remember, we were street kids who were running, jumping, hiding under cars, climbing rooves and an occasional tree in one of the parks (there weren't too many trees on our streets since we lived in an industrial area). In my younger years, with all of the people I hung out with, stayed with and played ball with, I never heard anyone say the infamous words, "I have nothing to do." Even if you were by yourself, in those days there was a game you could play.

Some of us were travelers and went to different parts of the neighborhood (which to us was practically a different world), to see what games they were playing and get those kids to play our games on our blocks. It could have been Stickball on First Street or going to Third Street Park to play softball – a new softball had the brand name "Clincher" on the leather covering that was sewn on, holding together the string that was wound around a sponge or some other round thing. And if the ball started to come apart, we just taped it back together to make it last longer because not too many of us had money to buy a brand new one; we were all poor, but none of us knew it. As far as I could remember, no one ever complained about getting hurt, we all tried to shake it off to get right back into the game again as quick as we could. We slid on concrete when we played softball or Stickball to make a base. In football, we jumped up into the air to make a tag on a kid who had the ball and landed on the concrete, sometimes on our chest or elbows without any padding. In all our games, there were plenty of scrapes, bumps and bruises but I can't remember anyone breaking anything (maybe I have a convenient memory). Our uniforms were dungarees, t-shirts, sweatshirts and Converse sneakers. We knew it was getting cold out when we landed on our feet while playing a game outside, our ankles would sting.

Tag

One kid is "It" and has to chase all of the other kids around to tag one of them. The one tagged is now "It" and has to tag any other kid to pass on being "It." This is probably one of the most basic games to play with another bunch of kids without needing any props or gear to play it. When you think about it, tag was kind of like passing on an illness or infection, making you "IT!" It wasn't uncommon for a kid being tagged to yell out that the "It" kid barely touched them, or needed to use both hands, or some other way of upping the ante, or changing the rules to keep from being "It."

Mumphreeze

We used to play Mumphreeze by choosing someone to be "it." Everyone would walk around until the "It" kid would yell out, "1, 2, 3, Mumphreeze!" then everyone had to freeze in place. If one of the kids moved, the "It" kid would yell out that kid's name, then everyone else would throw a beatin on the kid who moved, until that kid yelled, "1, 2, 3, Mumphreeze!" Of course, they'd yell as quick as they could, and surprisingly, no one grabbed that kid's mouth to keep him from yelling, "1, 2, 3, Mumphreeze!" If no one moved, then the "It" kid then walks around the frozen kids to see who moved. Any of the rest of the kids who were supposed to be frozen would try to throw a beating on the "It" kid when he wasn't looking and try not to get caught. This was a good way to get even with someone because we weren't always playing by the rules... unlike any other kid, EVER! There were plenty of times when everyone piled on the "It" kid and once no one was freezing when he'd yell, "1, 2, 3, Mumphreeze!," the game was over!

Freeze Tag

Everyone is running away from the "It" kid because as soon as you were tagged, you had to freeze right where you were. You could only be unfrozen or released by another kid who was still avoiding the "It" kid. Of course, the "It" kid was trying to get everyone frozen, so anyone trying to unfreeze anyone else was also being chased to be tagged.

Shadow Tag

This needed to be played on a sunny day because we were chasing each other's shadows to tag them using our feet by stepping on the shadow. If our shadows were short, like around noon, then it was hard to tag someone else's shadow.

Blindman's Bluff

The "It" kid was blindfolded, spun around and had to find the other kids without being able to see where he or she is going. One version was that all the other kids were supposed to stay in one place to even out the odds, but people slickly squirmed out of the path of the "It" kid to try to avoid being tagged. Another way to play it was that the blindfolded kid would get hit when he passed by the other kids – obviously, they could see him, but the blindfolded kid couldn't see all the other kids. The blindfolded kid would also try to peek under the blindfold, especially if it was a little loose and that would lead to people tying the blindfold too tight to avoid that from happening.

Hide and Seek

Another "It" kid game: The "It" kid would close his or her eyes and count to 10, or 50 or something that was announced when the game started. Everyone else would find a hiding spot. The "It" kid had to look for each of them. The last kid found is the winner. Sometimes the least popular kid was left hiding while everyone else left and went somewhere else. Kids can be terrible!

Hot Belt

This game was usually played with a garrison belt. How many of you remember a leather garrison belt? A garrison belt was usually a black belt that was used by cops, first responders and even us civilians (see the pictures below).

MAYBE GARRISON BELTS ARE A LITTLE THICKER THAN THE ONE(S) PICTURED

So, the kid who was "It" would hide this garrison belt while everyone else is turned away or covering their eyes. We played this on the street, so the belt could be hidden behind a garbage can, under a car, on a parked car's tire, or anywhere else on the street. Once the "It" person found a hiding spot for the belt, he'd turn around and say that he was ready or "ok." There was also always someplace designated as "base" or "homebase" where you were safe and couldn't be made "It" or in this case, you couldn't get the Hot Belt on your ass! Maybe the wall of a building or parked car, or a fence outside a house, or a Johnny-pump was "homebase." While all of the other kids hunted around looking for the belt, the "It" kid would either say, "so-and-so is hot [meaning that person is getting closer], or cold [because so-and-so is nowhere near the belt or moving away from where it is]." Whoever found the belt, can beat any of the rest kids playing the game and those kids had to run to "homebase" to be "safe" from that beatin! The last kid to make it to homebase was the next "It" kid who then hid the belt.

Kick the Can

One more game played with an "It" kid. Another kid throws a can as far as they could, and the "It" kid had to bring it back to "homebase," then count to ten while everyone else found somewhere to hide. "Homebase" most of the time was on top of a sewer. The "It" kid would look around for kids who were hiding, and whoever he saw, he'd yell out, "tap, tap, tap, so-and-so behind a car." If the "It" kid was correct, the kid who was spotted would go to a holding area and the only way kids got out of the holding area is if one of the other kids who were still hiding outruns the "It" kid to go kick the can off "homebase."

Boxball/Slapball

Another version of baseball on cement using a spalldeen, with only an infield line-up – a pitcher, 1st base, 2nd base, short-stop, 3rd base, catcher and a batter: everyone using only their hand to hit and field the ball. The infield would try to catch a fly-ball or field it, trying to tag the hitter out before getting to home plate to score a run, just like baseball.

Poisonball/Dodgeball

This was played with two teams. Again, a very simple game played with a Spalding (Spawldeen or spalldeen, that's what we called it) ball. The Spalldeen was thrown straight up in the air, and it had to hit the ground and bounce first, then both teams fought in a scrum (a crowd of kids who pushed and shoved to get at that ball), to get control of the Spalldeen. The side who had control of the ball throws it at kids on the opposing team. If the person who was targeted caught the ball, the person who threw it was out and control of the ball flipped sides. The person who was targeted was out; if they were hit with the Spalldeen and couldn't come back into that game, they had to wait for a new game to start. If the ball didn't hit anyone, then the team in control threw it again.

There was definitely some strategy to this game too. So, kids from the team without possession of the ball (let's call them Team A) would go onto the side with the opposing team (the kids in control of the ball, say, Team B), to try and catch it when it was loose, before Team B caught it again, just to keep things a little chaotic. Of course, once Team B got the ball back in their hands again, they'd throw it even harder at Team A, specifically targeting the kid(s) who tried to infiltrate. This would lead to people asking for mercy because it was a barrage coming at them from everyone on Team B without an end. Once someone asks for mercy, they are told to turn around as a kid from Team B basically used the ball to flog the backs of the legs of the kids who asked for mercy – on a cool autumn day, that ball stung like a mutha! So, I'm not sure we were all that merciful (kind of like the nuns and priests) … We went home after playing for a few hours and the welts on our bodies from getting whipped with that ball were legendary. This game was so engrossing that one time, on the only day of the week I worked as a grocery delivery boy (Saturdays, which was shopping day in our neighborhood), during my lunch break from 12p to 1p, I went looking for the game in our grammar school's schoolyard and played until the next thing I knew my father came looking for me because it was two o'clock and the delivery orders were piling up (well, maybe I did this more than once!). How many of you out there remember where you played this or a version of it?

Off the Point, A.K.A., Stoop Ball

One more game we played in our grammar school, school yard using the wall of the school with only a Spalldeen that we called "Off the Point." In different spots all over the school's walls, there were bricks protruding about two inches and each of us had our favorite brick we aimed the ball at to get a good, swift, ricochet when the ball hit that "Point," then we ran the bases just like in a traditional baseball game. Whoever you were playing against tried to catch the ball on a pop-fly or throw it to someone covering a base to tag you out when it wasn't a fly-ball; they were the team on the field. The kids throwing the ball "Off the Point" were basically a batter line-up, making up the opposing team.

"Stoop Ball" was something we played with the kids who lived on First Street, across from the school in houses with stoops that had steps, still using that Spalldeen; this sent us into the two-way traffic on First Street to cover and run the bases. You have to realize we lived in an industrial area; there weren't too many open spaces around us to make a proper baseball diamond, so we improvised. And at one point, our neighborhood had so many kids at the same time both schoolyards (our grammar school had two, a big one and a smaller one), were being used for something else, causing us to have no place to play. That's when we got creative and used the heads of different kids as "The Point" because that's how determined we were to play ball! And if you're wondering how the behavior of the ball was different: bonking it off a kid's head versus a wall or a stoop, well, it made the ball more unpredictable!!

Ice Cream Sticks/Hitting the Stick and Boxball/Hit The Penny

After eating an ice cream pop or a popsicle, we took the stick that was inside the ice cream or the ice, put it on the ground and then tried to hit it with a ball (usually *...a Spalldeen*) – or we used a penny or other coin instead of the ice cream stick. You had to throw and hit the stick or coin with the ball without a bounce to get a point. If you wanted to make it harder, you could increase the distance from the stick after each time you tried to hit it. So, for example, if you started out with the stick on the line in the cement sidewalk, and you were both on the next line out, each time you both threw the ball at the stick, you stepped back one pace each. You and whoever you were playing with would agree on what the winning score would be. I'm keeping this game alive because I just recently played it with my grandson using a coin, and he really enjoyed it. The teacher in me looked at this as a way to help develop his eye-hand coordination.

You could also play this without the ice cream sticks. Instead, you and your opponent would slap the ball back and forth in a volley between you both, using the lines of the boxes in the cement sidewalk for your boundaries or guides. The first person to miss gives a point to the other person. All in all, the poor-poor man's version of tennis.

Skelzies/Bottlecaps

Each person needed a bottlecap to flick or slide-snap toward one of the boxes on the Skelzies board that we drew with chalk on the ground. You couldn't just drag a bottlecap all the way to each box; the slide had to have enough initial momentum to make the bottlecap continue on for a few feet until it got near or made it in a box. We melted wax or crayons into our bottlecaps to make them a little heavier and even put a penny in it, then melt the crayon or a candle over the coin to add even more weight to keep the bottlecap on the ground, making it easier to aim at the square or at other people's bottlecaps to push them out of a box, kind of like Olympic curling. The Skelzies box we drew on the ground was sometimes in the middle of the street if there wasn't enough sidewalk, and there were 13 numbered boxes total. You had to slide your bottlecap into the first box, then the second, the third, and so on until you get your bottlecap into the center box, number 13. The 13th box had a poison-zone around it, that if your bottlecap went in there, you'd either lose turns, or stay there until another bottlecap hit you out of it. You could think of the poison zone as a mote.

BOTTLECAPS BEFORE BEING CUSTOMIZED
WITH WAX OR CRAYON

THIS IS HOW WE USED TO SEND BOTTLE CAPS
FROM ONE BOX TO ANOTHER, BY FLICKING THEM.

Tops

We Played It... Our Way!

First, we would choose by doing "One Potato, Two Potato" or eenie, meenie, miny, moe, or throwing our fingers out after choosing odds or evens... (I'll explain that later). The loser of "One Potato, Two Potato," eenie, meenie, miny, moe or odds/evens was the person whose top was put in the middle of a circle we drew in the street, on the tar. Someone else would launch their top from a standing position, by throwing it like a baseball (two fingers on the top of the top, the point of the top rested on the thumb), at the one in the street, with the string tied to their finger. If you hit the one in the street in the circle, you win. If your top missed the one you threw it at, and it was spinning, then you'd take your index finger and middle finger to slide it under the top to pick it up while it was still spinning to get it into the palm of your hand and to keep it spinning, then you'd bring it to the one in the circle, to throw yours at it again, trying to hit that top. If the top that belonged to the person who threw it at the one in the circle wasn't spinning, then their top went into the circle, and other people would throw their tops at it. The aim was to break the other person's top, so I'm sure you figured out that our tops did not last too long. The added benefit was that you'd humiliate the person whose top was in the circle... I told you we played it our way!

Odds/Evens

To choose up sides for a game, we threw out one or two of our fingers (index and middle fingers) and call either odds or evens. The two kids in charge of choosing up the sides faced each other and one kid would call odds while the other called evens. Then the two kids threw out their hand with one or both of those fingers out on each hand and whatever both kids' fingers added up to (an odd number or even number) determined who won. This was like a coin toss, without the coin. The winner got to choose first. When I was a young kid, I was usually picked last or close to it.

Football

We played two-hand-touch football in our grammar school schoolyard, which was all cement, so we'd either hit a wall or a fence if we were running and ran out of schoolyard! We played four-on-four, five-on-five, two-on-two or however many we had on each side. The ball is hutted or hiked to the quarterback, who was watched by some kid on the other team who was swinging his arms in the air, trying to interfere with the quarterback throwing a pass. The kid trying to interfere with that pass was giving a count of 3, 5 or 10, for the quarterback to either pass the ball or run with it, and wherever the quarterback got tagged was the new line of scrimmage. If the quarterback threw a pass that was completed and the guy who caught that pass got tagged, the new line of scrimmage was where the pass-receiver got tagged. If the quarterback made a pass and it was incomplete, the ball wouldn't advance, and that was the first of 4 downs. The ball not advancing meant that the play started at the same exact place on the field as the previous play. A down being an instance where the ball does not advance, and the team in possession of the ball has 4 times to advance the ball before the ball turns over to the other team, who goes through the same process as the first team.

Kings/Asses Up

We played with four or five guys, on the sidewalk with a wall of some building or another, or in the schoolyard against the school, with those protruding bricks. Each player stood in a box that was either drawn on the ground with chalk or we used the box outlines carved in the cement. The first box starting from the left was the King, then the Ace, then the Queen, going to the right, for as many players that were in the game.

The person in the King's box was in charge of the ball – the server – who threw it so it bounced on the ground in front of them in their box first, and then they made it hit the wall. Whosever box the ball landed in from off the wall from that serve, needed to slap it the same way, hitting the ground first in front of them, within their box and then bouncing against the wall to another player. Each person who didn't hit the ball the same way or who missed it got a strike against them, and each player had up to 5 misses, each miss or out, leading to spelling out the word "kings." Each time someone got an out, they'd be sent down to the end of the line (all the way to the right) to the farthest position. The person in the King box, the server, did not earn a letter if they missed, but after five misses, they got sent to the farthest position on the right. Sometimes people dribbled the ball between the ground and the wall, getting closer and closer to the wall, before they'd slice it, slamming it against the wall for it to go to someone they were trying to get out.

You could also run up to the wall and slap the ball as it was bouncing off the wall, before it bounced on the ground, to get the ball moving fast, and to catch someone off-guard who you wanted to get out. Sometimes when we sliced the ball with our hand, or chopped it, that put a spin on the ball, making it harder to predict where it was going and harder to hit then someone might slap the ball very softly, so there wasn't too much bounce and the person who needed to hit it, would get caught off-guard making it near impossible to hit the ball in time – maybe the kid would have to dive for the ball and get all scraped up trying to hit it because they hit the wall instead of the ball.

The lucky person who spelled out the word "kings" by getting out five times, was the loser who was then subjected to standing with their hands against the wall while the rest of us took turns throwing that spalldeen at their ass three times apiece: hence, Asses Up!

Buck-Buck/Johnnie on the Pony

First, there was the pillow, the kid standing with his back up against the wall who was supposed to be neutral, and the referee. Then there was the team of kids bent over at like a 90-degree angle, holding onto of the waist of the kid in front of them, and the kid in the very front who held onto the pillow. Another kid from the other team would take a running start and try to leap-frog across as many backs of bent-over kids he could, to get as far to the front as possible, to leave room for other kids on his team to do the same. The first kid to make the jump was usually the better athlete on the opposing team. If all of the other team made it onto the backs of the team bent over, then one of them had to hold up one or more fingers and say, "Buck, buck, how many fingers are up?" or "Buck, buck, how many horns are up?" Then the kid designated as, "the caller" on the bent-over kids' team tried to guess how many fingers were being held up, and the pillow verified if the guess was right.

If any of the kids who were jumping over the backs of the other kids touched the ground with their foot, that team was out, and then traded places with the bent-over kids. If the kids who were bent over, couldn't hold all of the weight of the kids jumping on their backs, they lost, and the other team could jump on their backs again. By that point, most of the time, the game was over; the kids who were bent over... were over it.

Red Rover

So there were two teams of kids with each side joining hands to form a line while facing each other. One side would say to the other, "Red rover, red rover, we call 'so and so' over!" The named kid would take a running start and run at the other team's line, trying to break through the chain of hands. If they don't break through, they'd join the other team. If the kid who was called does break through, they got to pick a kid from the opposing team to join them. This continued until there was one person left on one side who would be challenged to break the line of the team with all the kids, and if they broke through, they got to pick a kid to rejoin them and it would rebuild from there. If that one, lone kid does not break through, then that was the end of the game. Sometimes people holding hands when the kid who was called is running toward them at a good clip, to make that kid ram into something or fall! You had to watch!!

Paper Wrapper

We used to roll up an empty soft-pack wrapper that held cigarettes, and we swatted it with our hand as someone who was up against a wall pitched it to us, under-handed. If the kid who swatted the pack hit above one line that we drew on the wall, it was counted as a single. If the kid hit above the second line we drew, it was a double, and so on. If the pitcher caught what we swatted on a fly, it was an out. Another way to play baseball, using trash on the street this time. I played that game a lot with my friend Nunz.

Coco-Leave-E-O/Coco-O'Lere-E-O/Ring O-Leave-E-O

We chose up sides to make two teams. One side was defense and the other, offense. So the kids on offense would chase the kids on defense to grab each kid and hold onto him, then yell out, "Coco-Leave-E-O-1, 2, 3!" The kid who was caught was sent to a pen, or a den, or a jail until everyone on that team was caught. In the course of the game, kids on defense who were not caught would gauge if they could free everyone in the pen by running into it and yelling, "FREE!" and hope that the guards on the offensive team wouldn't be able to grab all of them to pull them back in. If all of the kids being chased get put into the pen, then the sides flip and they're now chasing the kids who had been chasing them.

Monkey-In-the-Middle

This was catch with one kid ("The Monkey") standing in between two other kids who were throwing the ball over the head of "The Monkey" in the middle. If the kid in the middle managed to intercept the ball, then the kid who threw the ball went into the middle. There were lots of other instances of people breaking the balls of a shorter kid, or younger kid or just some other unsuspecting target, where someone grabbed something that belonged to that kid, and the other kids threw it back and forth to each other, over the owner's head. My wife says her friends did that to her a lot because she was the youngest, so they grabbed her shoe or something else to throw around/ over her head. Someone would act like they were interested in something she had, grab it, then throw it to someone else while she was jumping up to try and intercept it or running to the kid about to throw it, usually without success! Ahhh, the good old days!!

Monkey Bars

We used to play this until we got tired. And guess what? It was another "It" game! The kid who was "It" would stand on the ground and count to ten or something. The rest of us ran to the monkey bars before he finished counting, then he'd climb up to try and catch us. Everyone swung all around, trying to avoid the kid who was "It" on these metal monkey bars that were on top of cement. Just about all of the local parks were completely paved and there was no padding underneath any set of monkey bars, so if you fell, you just needed to hope that you landed the right way, or you were screwed!

MONKEY BARS IMAGE, IS NOT INCLUDED BECAUSE THE PICTURE WE WANTED TO USE WAS FOR SALE AT ALL SORTS OF PRICES, DEPENDING ON THE USE.WE WEREN'T SURE WHAT THEY'D WANT IF IT WAS INCLUDED IN A BOOK...

Swings

Typically, every part was made out of galvanized steel, which included a two-and-a-half to three foot wide seat that was a bench with no back and chains holding the seat to the top of the frame. We sat on the seat and tried to get as high into the air as we could. When we were feeling really brave, we stood on the bench seat and swing as high as possible, sometimes until we were parallel with the ground or almost over the top of the frame. And again, there was no padding under those swing sets; if you fell, tough friggin luck! Ahhhhh-oooouch! The good old days!

Baseball Cards

There were two versions of playing with baseball cards. One was when we went into someone's hallway and flicked them toward a wall. The first card that landed on another, won all of the cards that were already thrown.

The other version is where, from a standing position, we each flipped the same number cards, maybe 10, for them to rotate in the air and land with either heads or tails showing. It was like a cross between a coin-toss and playing dice. The other kid had to match the same number of heads and tails cards to win all of mine, or I'd win all of his cards. So if I flipped 7 heads and 3 tails, and if the other kid flipped 4 tails, he didn't even have to finish, he just needed to hand over 10 of his cards because landing with more heads showing was the way to win. Let me tell you, if we knew then what we know now about the value of those cards today, whew! We had cards for Mickey Mantle, Willie Mays, Duke Snider, Gil Hodges... Those right there were worth a fortune a piece, and we were bending them, clipping them to our bicycle frames for all the spokes of the wheels to hit and make a sound like what we thought sounded like a motorcycle! What a sin!!

Simon Says

The "It" kid would say to the other kids, "Simon says..." and give an instruction to do something. The goal was to see who listened the best, because if an instruction was given without it beginning with, "Simon says..." and any of the kids did it anyway, they were out. The last kid who did only what "Simon said," was the winner. It was always fun to see who'd start following an instruction that didn't begin with "Simon says...," then catch themselves and try to stop before they were OUT!!

Mother, May I?

This game was the flip-side of Simon Says. One kid is "the Mother" and the rest of the kids are at a starting line. One by one, each kid asks, "Mother, may I take [whatever number] steps?" Or, "Mother may I skip?" or anything else. Mother either says, "Yes you may," or "No you may not." For the bunch of wild animals we were, to find ourselves asking, "Mother, may I?" is hilarious!

Redlight, Greenlight, 1, 2, 3

A bunch of kids playing outside with all but one lining up at a designated starting line. The one who's not with the rest is the lead kid and stands a few yards away with his or her back turned to all the other kids. The lead kid then decides whether to say to the other kids, "greenlight" or "redlight." If the lead kid says "greenlight," then all of the other kids could move around with the aim of reaching the lead kid. But as soon as the lead kid said "redlight," all of the other kids are supposed to stop moving, then the lead kid turns around quickly to see whoever was moving when "redlight" was called, and those kids are sent back to the starting line. It was great to see who had the most control of their own bodies to be able to stop, mid-action. The first kid to reach the lead kid wins the game and becomes the lead in charge of telling the rest of the kids, "redlight" or "greenlight." At some point, the kids sing out, "Redlight, greenlight, 1, 2, 3, but my wife and I can't remember when or why... Maybe *you* know??

Truth, Dare, Consequences, Promise or Repeat

This was really a dare game. A group of people had to pick one of the categories to do or say something. If you were given 'truth,' then when someone asked you a question, you were bound by honor to answer truthfully. If you were dared to do something, then honor binds you to take the dare and do what you were dared to do. It might be something like being dared to kiss the ugliest person or to chug a beer. As for 'promise,' you'd publicly promise something that your friends held you to. 'Repeat' was usually something humiliating that you had to say about yourself or about someone else that no one normally dared to fuck with, which set you up for quite the sitch later on. People were always finding something to pay someone else back for!

Spin the Bottle

Usually a group of boys and girls would sit in a circle with an empty bottle in the middle. Each person gets a turn to spin the bottle until it stops and whoever the bottle is pointing to, is the person to be kissed by the person who spun it. You could bet that when someone had a crush on someone else, that was the reason to start the game. The problem was when the bottle pointed at someone the spinner didn't like, or vice-versa – it could get a little awkward. In instances when the bottle landed on someone of the same sex, that was an automatic redo... at least in the circles I traveled in.

Seven Minutes In Heaven

This is a game where two people are chosen to spend "seven minutes in heaven," which meant they'd have to go to a dark room and do whatever they wanted. They could kiss, talk or whatever else they could think of. It was a convenient way to embarrass the two, maybe by forcing one kid into an intimate situation with an ugly or unpopular kid. Or making someone's girlfriend spend time alone with another guy who has a crush on her, and then watch the sparks fly later when the girlfriend gets asked about what happened by her boyfriend... Guys and girls being as immature as we were back then, (some never grew out of it), no answer was a good answer.

Stickball/Chopball/Eggball

There are lots of variations of Stickball, as you see in the above heading, all of which were the street-version of baseball. We used different parts of what was on the street like cars or in the street, like sewer caps/manhole covers (respectively), to make a baseball diamond. So, for example, homebase/homeplate or second base could be the manhole cover.

Second Base or Home Plate

First and third base was the tire of a car parked on either side of the street. The best Stickball court was on 1st Street, off Third Aven. The reason being was the street was a little wider (it was a two-way street!), so it gave us more field to play on. Also, there were no cars there because the whole area was zoned as commercial and didn't allow cars to park on the streets during certain hours. The teams were made up from different neighborhoods playing against each other, and kids on the teams and other people in the neighborhood were known to bet money on these games. The older guys' team was called the 7 Battlers, they were about ten years older than we were at that time. The unwritten law for the whole area was that on Sundays after church, we played Stickball.

We used to go to Pop's or Levine's, which was located on 5th Aven, between 5th and 6th Streets to buy patches to sew on or iron onto our shirts with what we chose for our team's symbol. Our team was the Four Aces, so we bought patches with four aces. We also bought letters to spell our names and numbers, all of these for our mothers to make our white T-shirts real team jerseys. Our mothers sewed or ironed the team symbol patch onto our left sleeves because most of us were right-handed and we wanted that symbol to face the team on the field when we were up at bat. We used these same t-shirts to play softball at Third Street Park on 4th Aven and 3rd Street, or at Fifth Street Park which was on 5th Street, between 4th and 5th Avens – that was down the street from P.S. 51, which was a shit-hole school. I recently heard about a kid who went to that school back then, and after his teacher failed him, the kid set the teacher's car on fire. Ironically, P.S. 51 is now highly sought-after!

Punchball/Fistball

This was played with a pimpleball (a white ball with all these pimples sticking out, all over it that was about the size of a softball), and it was like Stickball, but using your fist to punch the pimpleball and then run bases.

Hand-Slapping

This was more of an invitation for a beatin. One person held their hands out in front of them with their palms facing up, while the other person placed their hands on top – palm-to-palm. Each person would stare the other down. The person whose hands were palms up, tried to slap the tops of the hands of the person whose hands were palms down. Of course, the slapper had to be quick because the slappee would pull their hands away before they could be slapped. This built frustration to the point where pretty soon, the slapper just started slapping the other person in the head, and that never leads to anything good. I've morphed this into an exercise drill for kids just learning to swim as a way to show them how to arrange their hands with their fingers together to pull the water, instead of like a claw which gives hardly any momentum through the water for the swimmer.

Potsie/Hop-Scotch

So someone drew a grid of boxes on the sidewalk, with chalk, each box with a number from 1 to 10. You could look at this as a kid-level obstacle course. Each person got a turn to hop in the boxes. We used a Bobby-pin or a coin that we tossed into one box at a time, starting with the number one, and that was the box you had to skip while you hop into the rest of the boxes in number-order, landing with only one foot in each box. When you reached the end, you had to turn around in that last/tenth box on a single hop, then jump all the boxes again, this time in reverse order. The goal is to throw the 'stone' into each number and properly jump the rest of the boxes. If you missed a box, or you fell or hopped into the box with the bobby-pin, you'd lose your turn and have to start again from the beginning when it was your turn again. The first person to make it through this obstacle course by tossing the bobby-pin into all boxes from one to ten and hopping the empty boxes without missing, falling, or jumping into the box with the bobby-pin, wins.

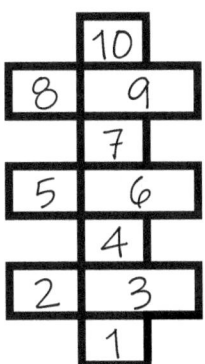

POTSIE/HOPSCOTCH BOARD WE'D DRAW ON THE SIDEWALK.

Unsupervised Play

From the 1960s through the 1970s, "white flight" (this was the term for the mass exodus of mostly white people who could afford to leave New York City to go to the suburbs and other parts of the country, which was one of the biggest reasons for the City going bankrupt in the 1970s – business development and slum-lords also contributed), led to empty lots all over the place and parts of the City that stayed undeveloped, which gave us kids opportunities to be a little wild. Anything that was abandoned or not properly locked up, we played there. The truck yard near the Gowanus Canal where a bunch of trailers or containers were left without anyone watching them is what we played hide and seek in, or we jumped from one trailer to another. None of these were open spaces designed for kids to play in; we were trespassing, which meant that sometimes we got chased, or worse, hurt.

My wife tells the story how in her neighborhood, there was a similar construction/truck yard, next to the N train line's 8th Aven stop. The gate around that site she said, was either unlocked or had a gaping hole they could climb through… or maybe the fence was just really easy to climb over – who remembers! At one point there was a dirt ditch that looked like it was dug to be the foundation of a building that wasn't built yet, but there was no concrete poured in it or anything else showing any other development, so it had a couple of feet of rainwater in it. On a summer day that was maybe in the 60s and over-cast, a bunch of her friends and her went into the yard, threw a couple of wooden pallets into what was now a small pond, grabbed a broomstick or two, paddled around like Tom Sawyer at the Coney Island bumper-cars (crashing them into each other), until her friend Scott decided to push and ram everyone else off the pallets into the mud water. Anyone who got wet stayed in those same clothes until going home for dinner because why should anyone let mud-drenched clothes dampen the day?? On a different day at that same truck yard, down a hill toward the trench where the N train ran, they noticed a couple of construction trucks that looked unguarded, so she and Scott got into one of the tucks and he managed to start it up (someone left the keys in the ignition). My wife was about 12 or 13 and Scott was about 15 or 16 at the time, which meant they had no friggin idea between the two of them how to operate a truck… With Scott behind the wheel, he had that truck jerking back and forth, making all sorts of noise that alerted the guard dogs because their barking started getting closer and closer to them in the truck. That's when they figured they should leave, so they jumped out of the truck and ran back up the 30-foot hill to the fence they came in through to avoid getting attacked. They barely made it out before the dogs got to the fence and whoever was in the construction trailer a few yards from the truck realized what was going on and came out. Sophia and Scott kept running for a few blocks without looking back in case the guy(s) at the site decided to chase them. Scott always found mischief for this bunch to get into: one of his cousins, a Hell's Angel, once called him "scutch." As for that lot, it eventually became a Citibank branch. Today, you would NEVER have a construction site or an area with building equipment left unattended like that; it was a completely different time.

Card Games

Maybe it's because of where I grew up, but there were lots of Card Games – if we weren't playing ball, we were playing cards:

Pinochle, Brisk, Rummy, One of the Three (which was the liars game), Acie-Ducie, 52-Pick-Up and Knuckles. I'm sure I'm forgetting something.

The way you got someone to play Knuckles was to have a few of you who knew what the game was, ask a person who didn't know, if they wanted to play it. Everyone would act all excited about it and ask, "You wanna play Knuckles?" trying to get this person caught up in your excitement to say 'yes.' Your follow-up was, "You ever play it before?" And, of course, no one wants to look stupid, so in trying to be cool you counted on them to say, "Oh yeah!" That's when you'd have the person make a fist, then you'd take a deck of cards and chop them on their knuckles with the side of the full deck a couple of times, and BOY, was it was painful! My wife thinks we also did this to the loser of some other card game. We got people to play 52-Pick-Up with the same kind of intro and then throw all the cards on the floor to have the other person pick them all up.

War

This game is played with an even number of people, but usually with just two, dealing the entire deck to the players face down. Once the dealing is done, each person turns over their top card and the rest stay face down. The person with the higher card wins the other person's card. If two players turn over the same value card, then it's War! Once War begins, the players blindly take out 3 cards from their own hand and put them face down in a neutral area between them. Then they draw a fourth card that they turn face up to see whose card is higher, and the higher card wins the three face-down cards from the other player as well as the one that started War. If there is another tie, then it's War all over again, with three more face-down cards and a fourth facing up until someone wins. The whole game is won when one person has all 52 cards.

JOBS

Ok, so here's something that's no surprise to anyone who knows me for more than five minutes, I pride myself on my work ethic. Well... because the people I admired in my life had two or three jobs (these days we call that multi-tasking). As a result, I felt if it was good enough for them, it's good enough for me. So my life-long relationship to working hard started with my first job when I was helping my grandfather, the super of "The Big Building" where we lived. He had me shoveling coal and cleaning the hallways on my own just based on his directions. That job was really about pleasing him, not really much else because it was for no pay, but the words, "Leonard, da bene." was all the payment I needed! And those old Italians threw around compliments like manhole covers, so that was big! You can read more about what I did for my grandfather in the "STORIES" chapter. I feel our generation and being Italian, I wasn't alone because for the most part, we were all trying to please our parents and grandparents and speak their language by working hard. To be honest and not egotistical, I can't remember ever not having at least two jobs and like I said, I didn't always get paid for them. So over my life I've had many jobs, and I've tried to never refuse any work offered to me because I would feel like I was doing something wrong, even now. It seems like the older I got, the more jobs I usually found myself working. A few years back, my wife was visiting with a relative of hers in Florida and when this aunt asked what I was up to, my wife told her, "He's working one of his six jobs." That aunt stared back at my wife and dead pan said, "Don't let him quit, he'll die!" At that particular time, I was teaching during the day, coaching in the afternoon and working as a bouncer at night at the country western bar owned by my two dear friends, Chardee and Tom. Anyway, I'm starting with the seeds of my work life from when I was young.

Lumper Boy

The next job I remember was when some of the guys in the neighborhood told us that there was a truck coming loaded with watermelons and they enlisted my friends and me to unload it. When the job was finished, we each got paid with a watermelon, so I took my pay home to my family. My father thought I stole the watermelon until I told him about the tractor-trailer (and I have no idea if those watermelons on that truck were stolen or not; all I know is that I was asked to do something, I did what was asked of me the way I was told to do it). He then looked outside and saw all of the other kids walking up the block with watermelons, and with that my grandfather interceded on my behalf, pointing out what my father saw outside, that all the other kids were also carrying watermelons to their houses. That settled the question in my dad's head and it was great; we all had watermelon for dessert after dinner that night. I felt so proud that I contributed to my family.

Shoeshine Boy

My next job was as a shoeshine boy (just because I still have it, ***don't ask me to get my shinebox***...!). I walked around my neighborhood carrying my shoeshine box, asking the men if they wanted a shine because they were always dressed with wingtips or what we called featherweight shoes. The only colors shoe polish and paste I had was black and brown. I also kept rags, brushes and two little pieces of cardboard inside that shinebox.

I FOUND MY SHINEBOX!! THIS IS THE VERY SAME SHOE SHINE BOX AND BRUSHES THAT I USED AS A LITTLE BOY, SHINING PEOPLE'S SHOES.

First step was that I'd put the cardboard in the shoe between the person's sock and the shoe to keep the polish and paste color from getting on the socks. Then, I applied the paste using the brush for it. After the paste came the polish that had its own brush and finally, I buffed the shoe with the rag, to give it as good a shine as I could. I think I charged a dime and a lot of the time, the customer would give me a quarter, so I got a fifteen-cent tip! I can't say how anyone else polished shoes, but this was how I did it and for me to get 150% over what I was charging as often as I did, must mean I was doing something right.

Grocery Delivery Boy

Next door to where I lived was Joe's Grocery Store, and I worked there as a delivery boy. The store had me use a 3 wheeled, wooden wagon to put the groceries in and make the deliveries around the neighborhood by foot pulling that wagon. One time during my hour break (I guess it was my lunch hour), I went over to the schoolyard where all my friends were playing Poison Ball (Dodge Ball with a Spalldeen), so of course I had to play too. Well, before I knew it, two hours went by and I only knew that because my father came looking for me. I don't know why it took him so long to figure out where I was because I was always in the schoolyard if I wasn't home or delivering groceries. When I got back to the store, there were a bunch of deliveries piled up, so I had to make up for my long break by making all those deliveries to everyone who was waiting – I think a few of them were my aunts. I got paid two dollars a day and I felt like I was rich – remember, this was about 1962, so two bucks was a nice amount of money to have.

Pin Boy

There was the time when I was a pin boy at our parish bowling alley. Believe it or not, bowling pins used to be placed at the end of the alley on the approach dots by an actual person. There was no machine pinsetter or pinspotter to do it, and I was one of the kids who placed them in that triangular pattern for the bowler to try and knock the pins down with a bowling ball. This was about 1965 or '66 in the basement of our parish grammar school where the gym was, and there were 6 alleys or bowling lanes that were open to the public with three pin boys manning two lanes a piece (the lanes were in pairs). From where we stayed in the back of the two lanes we covered, we used our foot to push a lever for the metal plates with metal spikes to come up from the floor, then place each wooden bowling pin on top of one of those spikes– the bowling pins had a hole in the bottom of them so they fit right on top of the metal spike that was sticking out of the floor for each of the bowling pins to be on the correct approach dot. When the bowler threw the bowling ball down the alley, their goal was to knock down as many of the pins as possible, trying to get a strike (where all the pins fell on the first try). The ball was supposed to roll down the alley with some force, but there were people (usually the men), who threw it at the pins like a baseball pitcher throws to a batter. The pins that were knocked down went into the pit behind the bowling pins (we were just off to the side of that), and us pin boys had to pick them up as well as any others that got knocked over next to the pins still standing on the approach dots when they didn't fall into the pit or the gutter. As for the bowling ball, we picked that up, put it on the long ramp (bowling ball return) from the pit that was angled for the ball to roll back to where the bowlers were (that wasn't motorized either). The ladies league was on Monday nights and there were some really bad bowlers. Sometimes when the ladies were bowling, we got impatient and couldn't wait to get out of the alley to go home, so we'd put up all the pins except the 5-pin, which goes right in the middle of the pack. Then when the women threw the bowling ball down the alley at the pins, from our place at the back of the lane, we pin boys would throw the 5-pin into the pins on the approach dots/triangle at just the right time to try to give them a strike so the game would end sooner. I don't know if any of them ever got wise to what we did...

Plenty of times, bowlers with strong arms crashed the bowling ball so hard into the pins that it was like an explosion, sending the pins into the air and hitting us pin boys in the legs, which come to think of it, the only time I was afraid of being a pin boy was when this guy Joe D. bowled. He would throw the ball so hard down the alley that the pins flew all over the place. My friend _Scooter_ brought that to my attention in a recent conversation we had. And as I think of it, I don't think any pin-boy ever got hurt bad doing this job, but it kept us on our toes.

MY WIFE AND I FOUND BOWLING PINS AT A MOTORCYCLE SHOP IN UPSTATE, NEW YORK, AND HERE I AM HOLDING THEM, BUT PROBABLY WITH A BETTER GRIP THAN WHEN I WAS A PIN BOY!

LANDMARKS

When I use the term landmark, I mean two things – places lots of people know and the ones no one knew about but were important to us because we lived, played and hung out in those places. Some people may have no idea what I'm writing or talking about, but in any case, this is the way I remember landmarks from my life.

1. First and foremost, the Big Building on Third Aven and President Street, the place I was born where two-thirds of the families in the building were my relatives. The Holy Grail of living (boy, if that building could talk...). And then the other Third Aven building, which was across the street from the Big Building that we moved into. Even though we lived in the other building for a short amount of time, it was memorable, especially because of Margaret (Mahgah-lad—phonetic Brooklynese-Italian pronunciation of Margaret, the way we spoke it in my neighborhood).

Margaret was 4 foot 9 inches tall, about 230 lbs or more, with a mouth like a truck driver, and a heart of gold. She had a dog that I'm pretty sure was named Lady, but the poor thing didn't know that was its name because Margaret always called it "Mother's C*nt!" We'll tell more Margaret tales in the "STORIES" chapter of Book 2 because there are so many and they're all great because of how wonderful she was! At some point, my friend Modz asked me if Margaret still had the dog, Mother's C*nt. I laughed my ass off because no one knew that dog's real name!

2.   Second was DeGraw Street which was where the homemade wine was made and where my paternal grandfather (who sold fruits and vegetables; the picture of my grandparents and me when I graduated from kindergarten is in the forward), raised Boxers. My cousin Andrew (Gimme Room), was born there. That's also the house where I wasn't allowed to go up to the second floor. When I was little, I would tap on the window and say to my grandfather, "Grandpa, Grandpa, watch this!" then I'd run through his rose bush trellis and get all cut up. My wife is typing this right now, laughing and asking me, "Why did you do that??" I can only shrug and say, "I don't know. Because it was there…"

3.   The Williamsburg Savings Bank building, the Brooklyn version of the Empire State Building. But when I was a kid, I actually thought that it was the Empire State Building.

4.   The parachute in Coney Island, the Eiffel Tower of Brooklyn.

5.   Golton's truck yard, where we used to play and throw these rubber tip things at one another (no one was really sure what they were). They were about an inch long and circular, but I can't tell you much more than that.

163

6.   The Gowanus Canal, or Lavender Lake – Brooklyn's Venice. We used to play in the empty trucks in the truck yard right next to the canal. We jumped from truck roof, to truck roof, to truck roof. One time, one of my friends missed the roof he was jumping to and fell, bouncing or ricocheting off the two trucks he fell between until he hit the ground, a good ten/ twelve-foot drop, but he wasn't hurt (don't ask me how that was possible). I remember my daughter Louise was in Pennsylvania at cheerleading camp, and some of the parents were talking about the camps they went to as kids when I piped up to mention my camp being the Gowanus Canal … they looked at me like I had four heads and started to step away from me (I think they were wondering if I might be radio-active).

The Gowanus Canal was known as Lavender Lake to those of us who lived near it. It's the same canal where I took this girl Rita for a make-out session when we were teenagers! That canal was infamous, especially in Brooklyn. My wife said that when she used to take the express bus from Bay Ridge into Manhattan and closing her eyes to try to get a little extra sleep on the way to her office, she knew when the bus was going over the canal because of the stench – it was a like a slap in the face awake! You can't imagine how intense that smell was on those dog-days of summer, but that was our summer camp! My friend Dave the Dude always said that anyone who lived too close to it was shot, that there was no help for them because the canal rotted or cooked their brain. My friend Buckwheat said that about my son. Then, the city, in all its wisdom, discovered that there was a fan at the end of the canal that was broken and once they fixed it, NO MORE STENCH because the water was moving again! It's now a superfund site that the EPA is cleaning up... but I'm dumbfounded because now people go kayaking in that canal! There is a whole history of massive industrial dumping and legends of bodies, cars and whatever else nobody wanted that wound up at the bottom of that canal. Those of us who grew up around the canal can blame it for rotting our minds and making us fucked up; what's the excuse for the new-comers... kayaking?

7.   DeGraw St. Park at Third Aven and DeGraw St. When I was a kid, that was the park we went to, to go into the sprinklers. It was also two blocks away from where my father was born.

8. Two-Tom's, I'm sure everyone in creation knows where Two Tom's was – it's closed down now – and their infamous three-inch thick (maybe thicker) steaks and chops. I lived a block from Two-Tom's. When we were kids, we used to chip in our money together to get two pies and two sodas from Two-Tom's and sit in their backyard.

Whatever money was left over, we went next door to Tanny's candy store. Tanny and his wife were two of the few Jewish people in our neighborhood and they took care of us in terms of candy.

9. **Tip-Top Stadium, on 3rd Aven and 1st Street, where the Dodgers played baseball, NOT Ebbets Field. The walls of Tip-Top Stadium are still there.

10. Steeplechase Park in Coney Island. I'm sure everyone (of a certain age) has a story about Steeplechase like the electric horses, the clown that slapped you on the ass with a ruler to get you to go down the slide, onto the spinning floor, and the spinning barrel that you had to walk through while in the funhouse. Unfortunately the park closed in 1964.

11. Benny's Candy Store on Third Aven, where we used to listen to music like The Wanderer by Dion and He's So Fine by The Chiffons.

12. The Recreation Center of our grammar school, where every day except Wednesdays (because that was ladies' bingo night) and Sundays, we spent all our time there and in the schoolyard just outside. We played poison ball, softball, Coco Allevio, and anything we could do outside, all in that schoolyard. Again, there had to be fifty, sixty kids hanging out in the Recreation Center/gym, or in both the big and small schoolyards.

13. When I was a kid, I liked to watch Vic the Blacksmith shoe the horses. His shop was on Third Aven between Carroll and First Streets. He was about 5'3, tough as nails, and to be honest with you, I thought he was actually eating nails because of how he used to hold them in his mouth. Vic also had his Italian stogie, or stinker (does anyone remember DeNoble cigars?) in one side of his mouth and the nails he shod the horses with on the other. He had no magnet on his heavy, thick leather apron like what they have today. But let me tell you, Vic definitely had a way with horses.

14. There was also a stable next to Vic the Blacksmith's shop where this guy Tom owned horses that he rented out to people in the neighborhood. There were plenty of Saturday afternoons when I spent my time with Tom's horses and across the street at George's chicken market.

15. George's Chicken Market was where they used to kill fresh chickens, and it was quite the process! Of course I used to watch it, but I won't describe it here since we're so far removed from how animals are processed for food consumption that it might be hard to... digest!

16. On Third Aven and Carroll Street, there used to be a barber shop where I got my first haircut. That's one that I don't remember its name.

17. Sunset Park. We used to walk up to Fifth Aven, take the B63, get off at 42nd St. (in Brooklyn), walk into the park and cool ourselves off for the day in the public pool there. How many of you knew the Sunset jingle? (See "TRIVIA" chapter).

18. We went to Raven Hall in Coney Island when we were kids, if we didn't go to the beach, Steeplechase Park, or Sunset Park. The Ravenhall amusement park was one more choice for us.

19. Otto's Candy Store on President Street, between Third Aven and Nevins Street, where we used to play cards and hang out. Like I said, if we weren't playing some sort of ball game somewhere, we played cards.

20. Long after the New York ice kings of the 19th century and up until the 1920s, we still had the Knickerbocker Ice Plant on President Street between Third and Fourth Avens; they sold ice by the block and bagged ice. You put the money in the coin slots of the ice machine, pushed the lever, and your choice of ice came out. It was a big warehouse and some of us knew the maintenance guy who, rather than see us hang out on the street, he used to let us into the ice plant, where we played cards and drank beer. There were times we tried to steal the ice by crawling up the shoot and pulling it down, right Bobby? What a bunch of ingrates we were!

21. Across the street from The Village Inn was a bar called The Magic Touch on Third and Hoyt Streets. Till this day, the sign that says The Magic Touch still hangs on the building.

22. There were two butchers in our neighborhood: Johnny the Butcher who was on Carroll Street off of Third Aven (next to Farmer Jones' Grocery store). The other was Charlie's Butcher Shop, on Third Aven between Union and President Streets, next to Two-Tom's. The funny thing I remember about Charlie's butcher shop was that he had a chicken running around there – you can bet the Board of Health would fine the crap out of him if he had a live farm animal running around in his shop today.

23. I started my formal education in Catholic grammar school as a kindergartener in 1955 and stayed until I graduated in 1965. I

remember that first day of kindergarten when all the kids left their mothers and fathers, and went right to their seats in the classroom. But I left my mother's hand and went straight to the piano, then started playing it. I had a lot of trials and tribulations at my grammar school that are detailed in the "STORIES" chapter.

24. Downtown Brooklyn had a ton load of clothing and other kinds of stores that were pretty notable like A&S (Abraham and Strauss which got bought up by Macy's) and May's clothing stores. Florsheim Shoes and the F. W. Woolworth food counter where we used to get fantastic fried chicken. Then there was Junior's, on Flatbush Aven Extension and Dekalb Aven. Not sure when they became the huge juggernaut they are today, but they were there when we were growing up and were always known for their cheesecakes.

25. 215 Montague St., that's where Jackie Robinson signed his first contract to play for the Brooklyn Dodgers on August 28th, 1945. I don't know if a plaque is on the actual building, but if it isn't, it should be.

26. The Bosset Hotel, that's where the Brooklyn Dodgers celebrated their World Series victory in 1955.

27. Ebbitt's Field, at 55 Sullivan Place, near Flatbush Aven and Empire Blvd., where the Dodgers, with Jackie Robinson, won the 1955 World Series.

28. The Brooklyn Museum, our own piece of world culture.

29. The Brooklyn Botanical Gardens, which are absolutely beautiful. People have their weddings there.

30. Prospect Park, our woods in the middle of our urban jungle. I think the same guy who designed Central Park in Manhattan, Olmsted, did Prospect Park too.

31. Mary's Grocery Store and across the street, Joe's Grocery Store, both on 3rd Aven and President Street. To no one's credit, we used to call Joe's, "Joe the Jew," even though he was Italian like the rest of us. And I have no idea how he got that name, I just know that's what everyone called him.

32. John's Candy Store on Carroll Street between 3rd Aven and Whitwell Place.

Movie houses

1. Garfield

2. Avon

3. Prospect

4. The Fox Theater

5. The Terminal

6. Paramount

7. Albee

8. Duffield

9. Saunders

10. Alpine

11. Marlboro

12. The Fortway

13. The Dyker

TRIVIA

Ok all you Baby Boomers (and don't give me that, "OK boomer!" line…), I'm going back to a far better place, when we were young, innocent and could get away with almost anything! But now ponder this, for anyone born from 1948 to 1952, according to a couple different sources during that time period:

- The average new home cost $8,450

- Average yearly household income was $3,220

- Rent was $75 a month

- Gas was $0.18 per gallon – oh man!!

- Milk, $0.84 a gallon

- Eggs were $0.24 a dozen

- One pound of chop-meat (beef) was $0.49

To me, being that I was born right, smack in the middle of the 20th Century in 1950, a nice round number, we didn't know what was in store for us, so it was a time of innocence for those of us who were kids back then. But looking back at headlines and the history of that time, the world around us was nowhere near innocent – what did we kids know? So you could debate if it was a time of innocence or just plain ignorance for us kids (or maybe plausible deniability!!). All we knew back then was that we just wanted to get through our school days and to the next ballgame in the schoolyard or to an abandoned lot to explore and find some mischief. It was a time when all we had to worry about was crossing the street and it made a big difference if it was a small street or a big street for when our parents allowed us to cross on our own; otherwise, remember, we had to get permission! The time we were supposed to go home was basically when the streetlights came on. If the girl we liked said 'yes' when we asked her out, it was the best thing ever! There were a few other things that maybe each of us as individuals remembers… and here are some more:

- We made carpet guns and zip guns; I just found out zip guns were also called "improvised firearms."

Carpet guns were made with a long two-by-four, a nail, a clothes pin and a rubber band that acted as a sling-shot to shoot some scavenged projectile (for more about these, see the "TRADITIONS" chapter).

We made a zip gun by mounting the bottom part of an old car antenna or a tube with heavy-duty rubber bands as a make-shift gun barrel that a small bullet could slide through, on a piece of a two-by-four that you could hold in your hand, with a latch at the 'loading' end of the antenna to slap the bullet or another projectile through the tube, also using a rubber band for the sling-shot action. The below picture shows the type of bullets we used for a zip gun.

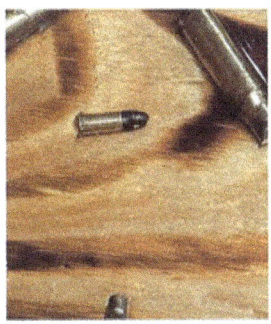

THE LINK BELOW HAS A PICTURE OF WHAT A VERSION OF A ZIP GUN LOOKS LIKE:
https://www.thefirearmblog.com/blog/2019/05/30/improvised-firearms-zip-guns-like-grandpa-usedto- make/
IT'S PROBABLY A SIGN OF THE TIMES BECAUSE I DON'T THINK KIDS TODAY NEED TO IMPROVISE ANY OF THIS, SOMEHOW REAL GUNS ARE PRETTY EASY TO COME BY.

- We also made old–fashioned sling-shots – I'm sure I don't need to describe them.

- King of the Hill, we pushed other kids off the hill that we claimed (see the "TRADITIONS" chapter), especially when it snowed a lot. Sanitation cleared the streets of the snow for cars to be able to drive down without getting stranded in a snowdrift, and they pushed the snow into these mounds or hills next to sidewalks.

- We tanned on tar-beach, well, not me so much. But tar-beach was usually the roof of an apartment building. It was bigger than someone's house roof and easier to access because no one's parents were in charge of stopping us from going up there for one thing. One of our friends in college fell asleep with his arms over his head and his legs splayed wide open while he was sunbathing on tar beach. So to break balls, everyone else that was with him left him there, spread-eagle. When our friend woke up, he couldn't put his arms

173

down or walk right because of how sunburned he was between his legs and under his arms; it was like he just got off a horse and was ready to "draw!" (Look! It's a cowboy reference! More to come...).

Now I hope you ladies don't get mad because in parts of this great chapter, and the rest of the book, I write as a young boy who liked cowboy shows and other boy-centric activities and programs – I really can't remember all that many shows geared toward girls (my wife asked me this very question), but what I do remember is further on down...

TV was a main-stay in our lives because we were the first generation that grew up with it, and Saturday mornings were especially important because we had our heroes: the cowboys and their shows. Gene Autrey, Hopalong Cassidy, and as my grandfather used to call him, Royale Rogers (that's how he said Roy Rogers in his unique broken-English), and many, many more. One of the main reasons we liked cowboys was because they were the heroes, the good guys, and all kids love good guys. My mother's father was off-the-boat from Italy and LOVED cowboy movies; for some reason he felt a strong connection to them. Maybe because cowboys were portrayed as men of their word, just like he was, and I carry that bond today, every day, and all of my life. Now how many of you know what I'm talking about?

Weekend afternoons were when the "Million Dollar Movie" was on TV. Anyone remember that? And who remembers the theme to the Million Dollar Movie? Don't forget, we had only seven or eight stations, can you name them? Not such a hard question – channels 2, 4, 5, 7, 9, 11, the infamous Channel 13 if you had a decent antenna, and Channel 21 if your antenna was industrial strength! No one heard of cable because it didn't exist. All television stations signed off at about 2 a.m., with the playing of the National Anthem followed by just white snow on the screen with that white noise sound (HBO does that for a brief moment before it airs one of its own programs, maybe as an ode to that bye-gone-era).

Let's go on and see how many TV shows and movies you remember, and the people that were in them (answers will be in the back of this chapter).

Let's start with westerns and the like

"The Life and Time Of Wyatt Earp"

1.   Who played Wyatt Earp?

2.   Who was Wyatt Earp's side-kick and what was his occupation?

3.   The theme and music throughout the early episodes of "The Life and Times of Wyatt Earp" were a group of acapella singers; what were they called?

"The Adventures Of Wild Bill Hickok"

4.   Who played Wild Bill Hickok?

5.   What was Wild Bill's partner's name?

6.   What were their horses' names?

"Bat Masterson"

7.   Who played Bat Masterson?

8.   The actor who played Bat Masterson was in another series; what was it called?

"Track Down"

9.   Who played in Track Down?

10.   The actor who played in "Track Down" was in another series; what was it called and who played his partner in this series?

"Have Gun, Will Travel"

11.   Who played in "Have Gun Will Travel"?

12.   What was the name of the lead character in "Have Gun Will Travel"?

13.   Do you know the words to the theme song?

"Maverick"

14.   Who played in "Maverick"?

15.   What were the words to the theme song of Maverick?

"The Riffleman"

16.   Who starred in "The Riffleman"?

17.   What professional sports teams did the lead actor play on?

18.   What was the lead character's name?

19.   What was the name of the town where "The Riffleman" took place?

"Hopalong Cassidy"

20.   Who played Hopalong Cassisdy?

21.   Name Hopalong Cassidy's three side-kicks

22.   What was Hopalong Cassidy's horse's name?

"Wanted Dead Or Alive"

23.   Who played in "Wanted, Dead Or Alive"?

"Davy Crockett"

24.   Who played Davy Crockett? Was Davy Crockett known by other names?

25.   Who was Davie Crocket's sidekick and who played the role?

26.   What other two TV series did the actor who played Davy Crockett's sidekick star in?

27.   What were the words to Davie Crocket's theme song?

"Roy Rogers"

28.   What was the name of Roy Rogers' wife?

29.   Name Roy Rogers' ranch

30.   What song was at the end of each "Roy Rogers" episode?

31.   What were the words to Roy Rogers' theme song?

32.   What was the name of Roy Rogers and his wife's horses?

33.   Name Roy Rogers' side-kick and the side-kick's vehicle and what type of vehicle was it?

34.   What was the name of Roy Rogers' dog?

"Lone Ranger"

35.   Who was the Lone Ranger's side-kick?

36.   What were the names of The Lone Ranger and his side-kick's horses?

37.   Do you remember the narration before each "Lone Ranger" episode?

38.   How did each episode of "The Lone Ranger" end?

"Cisco Kid"

39.   Who played the Cisco Kid and his partner?

40.   What is the Cisco Kid's partner's characters' name?

41.   Can you recite the introduction of "The Cisco Kid"?

42.   What was the Cisco Kid's and his sidekick's horses' names?

43.   How did the Cisco Kid end each program?

"The Rebel"

44.   Who starred in "The Rebel"?

45.   What was the name of the lead character in "The Rebel"?

46.   What was the theme song of "The Rebel"? Who sang "The Rebel" song?

"Lawman"

47.   Who played the lead in "Lawman"?

48. What was the name of the deputy in "Lawman" and who played him?

49. Starting in season 2, what was the name of the saloon that the characters of "Lawman" went into and who owned it?

"Gunsmoke"

50. What town did "Gunsmoke" take place in?

51. Who played the sheriff on "Gunsmoke"?

52. Who were the deputies on "Gunsmoke" and who played them?

53. What was the name of the saloon on "Gunsmoke" and who owned it?

54. Who was the blacksmith on "Gunsmoke"?

The Range Rider

55. Who played the Range Rider?

56. What was his theme song?

More About Cowboys

57. What was the first cowboy **movie** (no, not a TV show)?

58. Name the cowboy who carried a whip

59. Name the singing cowboy, theme song and horse's name

60. Who was one of the first, if not _THE_ first on-screen cowboy?

61. What cowboys dressed in black?

62. Can you name three dogs that were in TV series?

63. Name three TV series that had horses in them

64. Who played in Sea Hunt (a kind of a western under the sea)?

Kids shows

Remember "Howdy Doody?" I feel like it was (for most of us), the first children's show; this and "Captain Kangaroo." There were lots of others that followed, like Soupy Sales, Sheri Lewis and Andy's Gang, to name a few.

65.   What were the kids in the stands on "Howdy Doody" called?

66.   Name five characters on "Howdy Doody"

67.   When did "Howdy Doody" air?

The Little Rascals was a repackaging of the Our Gang short films that were produced from 1922 until 1944. In the early TV age, these shorts became The Little Rascals. The characters were a little more real, almost as real as us, and always getting into mischief. They had one dog that hung out with them; we had two with us.

68.   What was the name of their mule and dogs?

69.   Who was the cop?

70.   Name the two fat kids on the "Little Rascals"

71.   What was their sign

72.   What was Chubby's real name?

73.   Name the three teachers – yes, there were three that I could remember…

74.   Did you ever see one of the teachers?

"Mickey Mouse Club"

75.   Name five members

76.   What were they called?

77.   Can you sing the theme song?

78.   Who was Mickey's girlfriend?

Looney Tunes

79.   Name five characters (or more if you can)

80.   Name the two crows

"Batman"

81.   Who played Batman?

82.   Robin?

83.   Butler?

84.   Name seven villains – 10 for extra credit

"Superman"

85.   What was Superman's real name

86.   Name the characters

87.   What was the editor's famous saying?

88.   What was the name of the Newspaper where the characters worked?

89.   What was the inspector's name?

90.   How did Superman open? What was the introduction?

"Leave it to Beaver"

91.   Name the family

92.   Name the pain in the ass

93.   The school Beaver went to

94.   The teacher

"Dennis the Menace"

95.   What was his trademark?

96.	What other character in a child's program had the same trademark?

97.	What was his neighbor's name?

"Andy's Gang"

98.	What were the three animals on Andy's Gang?

99.	Who played Andy?

100.	What were the words to the theme of Andie's Gang?

Kids Show Hosts

101.	Name these three hosts: the Merry Mailman, the cop and the sailor

Comedies/Early Sit-Coms

Who remembers the "Bowery Boys?"

102.	What other name did they go by?

103.	Name the main five Bowery Boys

104.	Name the candy store owner

Okay, guys, how many of you remember "Amos and Andy?"

105.	Aside from Amos and Andy, how many characters can you name?

106.	What was the name of their club/fraternity?

107.	One of them was married; who was it and what was his wife's name?

"Abbott and Costello"

108.	Who was their landlord?

109. What was the cop's name?

110. Lou's best friend?

111. Monkey's name?

112. Fruit peddler's name?

113. Lou's girlfriend's name?

"The Honeymooners"

114. What were the names of all the characters on the show?

115. What was the lead character's job?

116. Who was the lead character's best friend?

117. Where did they all live? What was the street name? Is that really a street in that neighborhood?

118. What was the name of their lodge?

"The Life Of Riley"

119. Who played Riley?

"Beverly Hillbillies"

120. Name of the four hillbillies

121. Name the banker

122. Sing the theme

123. They went to Beverly Hills, but where did they come from originally?

My Little Margie

124. Who played Margie?

125. Who played Margie's dad?

126. What was the name of Margie's boyfriend?

"Our Miss Brooks"

127.   Who played Miss Brooks?

128.   What other sit-com did the lead actress play in?

129.   What was Miss Brooks' occupation?

"Topper"

130.   Who starred in the TV version of Topper?

131.   Who was in the 1937 movie?

"The Many Loves Of Dobie Gillis"

132.   Who played Dobie Gillis?

133.   Who was Dobbie's side-kick/best friend?

134.   What was the stage name of Dobbie's best friend?

135.   What was Dobbie's best friend?

136.   What else did the actor who played Dobbie's best friend play in (he was especially noted for one role, and a less-known role as well)?

"Real McCoys"

137.   Name the characters on the show

138.   Their helper

139.   Sing the theme song

"Green Acres"

140.   Name some of the main characters on the show

141.   Sing the theme song

"My Three Sons"

142.   Who was the actor who played the father?

143.   Who was the uncle, who also played in another sitcom

144.   Name the dog

145.   Name all the sons

"I Love Lucy"

146.   What was the name of their corporation?

147.   What was Ricky's job?

148.   What was Ricky known for?

149.   Name the landlords

150.   Where did they live?

The Munsters

151.   Can you name the Munsters?

152.   What was their address?

How many of you had lunch with Soupy Sales, better known as Uncle Soupy?

153.   What was his trademark?

154.   What was the New Year's Day incident?

155.   What were the animal characters who appeared in the show?

156.   Do you rememba his song?

"I Dream Of Genie"

157.   Who was the star of "I Dream of Genie?"

158.   And who was her master?

Police Shows

"Highway Patrol"

159.   Who played in Highway Patrol?

"M Squad"

160.   Who played in M Squad

"77 Sunset Strip"

161.   Who played in "77 Sunset Strip?"

162.   Do you remember the song about one of the characters?

"Dragnet"

163.   Who played in Dragnet?

164.   Who were the main character's two partners?

165.   Do you remember the introduction?

166.   What was the last thing on that show?

"The Fugitive"

167.   Who played the fugitive?

168.   Cop that was chasing him

The Saint

169.   Who was the star?

170.   What movie role was the star also known for?

Peter Gun

171.   Who was the star?

Barretta

172.   Who was the star?

173.   What other series did he play in when he was a child?

Mod Squad

174.   Who was in the cast?

175.   What were the character names?

176.   What was the name of their commander?

Variety Shows

177.   Name five variety shows.

178.   Name music/teen-oriented variety shows

179.   Who wrote for a 1960s comedy/variety show and, in the 1970s, guest-hosted multiple episodes of a comedy/sketch variety show before moving on to movies?

Ventriloquists

180.   Name 3 ventriloquists

181.   Name the dolls used by these ventriloquists

Miscellaneous Trivia

182. Name 5 movies with key or iconic scenes or mostly filmed in Brooklyn (some were also filmed in other boroughs too)

183. Name five Drake's Cakes

184. How many cigarette brands can you name that don't exist now?

185. What cigarette slogan was, "I'd rather fight than switch"?

186. What cigarette ad said that they'd "Walk a mile..."?

187. What commercials was the character Josephine, the plumber, in?

188. Name the three television programs that June Lockhart played in

189. Name the three programs Harry Morgan was in

Jingles and Themes

190. Do you know the Pepsodent jingle?

191. What beer was the champagne of bottled beer?

192. Do you remember any beer commercial jingles?

193. Do you remember Nestles theme?

194. What kind of animal sang the Nestlé's commercial jingle?

195. Mr. Clean theme

196. What was the Good N Plenty jingle?

197. Do you remember the jingle for Bonomo's Turkish Taffy?

198. Ipana Toothpaste: who/what was the spokesman and what was the theme?

199. What hair care product had the slogan, "A little dab'll do ya"?

200. What did Vitalis have?

201. What was the women's version of Vitalis?

202.   Do you remember Chunky? What was the slogan and who was the spokesperson?

203.   Name fifteen candies from when we were kids

204.   Can you sing the Chock Full O Nuts jingle?

205.   Are you familiar with G & D Sweet Vermouth; do you remember what those initials stand for? Do you remember their commercial and what the spokesperson said?

206.   What is the mascot of Wise Potato Chips?

207.   Who was the host of You Bet Your Life?

208.   Who was the original host of What's My Line?

209.   Who was famously fired on air in 1953, and who fired that person?

210.   Who ended "Merry Melodies," and what was the closing line?

211.   Sunset Park jingle

What discontinued product, show, piece of clothing, custom, or anything else would you like to see come back? For me, I'd like to see Charlotte Russe treats, and old candy stores with penny candies and those big soft pretzels that we picked ourselves, putting our hands all over every pretzel on top, to get to the one at the bottom of the stick because it had the most salt. Also, in those old candy stores was an awesome jukebox, 2 plays for a dime and 6 for a quarter. They had about 200 selections, which at the time was the closest we had to a D.J. These machines were the next step after player pianos and we loved them. The jukeboxes were usually Wurlitzer, Seeburg Select-O-Matic, Rock-Ola and AMI/Rowe:

Answers

1. Hugh O'Brien

2. Doc Holiday, Dentist

3. Ken Darby Singers

4. Guy Madison

5. Jingles, played by Andy Devine

6. Buckshot and Joker

7. Gene Barry

8. Burke's Law

9. Robert Culp

10. "I-Spy" with Bill Cosby

11. Richard Boone

12. Will Paladin

13. "Have Gun Will Travel
    Reads the card of a man
    A night without armor in a savage land
    A soldier of fortune is a man called Paladin
    Paladin, Paladin, where do you roam?
    Paladin. Paladin, Paladin,
    Far, far from home"

14. James Garner and Jack Kelly

15. Who is the tall, dark stranger there?
    Maverick is the name
    Ridin' the trail to who knows where
    Luck is his companion
    Gamblin is his game
    Smooth as a handle on a gun
    Maverick is the name
    Wild as the wind in Oregon
    Blowin' up a canyon
    Easier to tame

Riverboat, ring your bell
Fare thee well, Annabel
Luck is the lady that he loves the best
Natchez to New Orleans
Livin on jacks and queens
Maverick is a legend of the West

Riverboat, ring your bell
Fare thee well, Annabel
Luck is the lady that he loves the best

Natchez to New Orleans
Livin on jacks and queens
Maverick is a legend of the West
Maverick is the legend of the West!

16.   Chuck Connors (if you also knew he was from Sunset Park, Brooklyn, you're really "in the know")

17.   Chicago Cubs 1951 and Boston Celtics 1947–48

18.   Lucas McCain

19.   North Fork, New Mexico Territory

20.   William Boyd

21.   California and Lucky and Edgar Buchannan

22.   Topper

23.   Steve McQueen

24.   Fess Parker, King of the Wild Frontier

25.   George Russel, played by Buddy Ebsen

26.   "The Beverly Hillbillies" and "Barnaby Jones"

27.   "Davie, Davie Crocket
King of the wild frontier
Born on a mountain-top in Tennessee
Greenest state in the land of the free
Raised in the woods
So he knew every tree

Killed him a bear when he was only 3
Davie, Davie Crocket
King of the wild frontier"

28.   Dale Evans

29.   Double R

30.   "Happy Trails"

31.   Happy trails to you
      Until we meet again
      Happy trails to you
      Keep smilin' until then
      Who cares about the clouds when we're together?
      Just sing a song and bring the sunny weather
      Happy trails to you
      'Till we meet again

32.   Trigger and Buttermilk

33.   Pat Brady, Nellybelle and a Jeep

34.   Bullet

35.   Tonto

36.   Silver and Scout

37.   **Narrator:** "A fiery horse with the speed of light, a cloud of dust and a hearty, 'Hi Yo Silver!' The Lone Ranger!"
      Lone Ranger: "Hi Yo Silver, away!"
      Narrator: "With his faithful Indian companion Tonto, the daring and resourceful masked rider of the plains led the fight for law and order in the early west. Return with us now to those thrilling days of yesteryear. The Lone Ranger rides again!"

38.   "Hi yo Silver, away!"

39.   Duncan Renaldo

40.   Pancho, played by Leo Carrillo

41.   "Here's Adventure, Here's Romance, Here's O'Henry's Robinhood of the west, the Cisco Kid"

42. Diablo and Loco

43. "Goodbye Amigos." "See you soon, Ha!"

44. Nick Adams

45. Johnny Yuma

46. "The Rebel – Johnny Yuma", Johnny Cash

47. John Russell

48. Johnny McKay, played by Peter Brown

49. There were two of them, the Blue Bonnet and the Bird Cage, Lily owned the Bird Cage

50. Dodge City, Kansas

51. James Arness played Matt Dillon

52. Festus, played by Ken Curtis, and Chester, played by Dennis Weaver

53. Long Branch, Miss Kitty

54. Quint Asper, played by Burt Reynolds

55. Jock Mahoney

56. Home On the Range

57. The Great Train Robbery

58. Lash LaRue

59. Gene Autry "Back In The Saddle Again" and Champion / Roy Rogers was "Happy Trails" and Trigger (Golden Cloud was before Trigger)

60. William S. Hart was the first on-screen cowboy, but Tom Mix was the first western star

61. Lash LaRue, Hopalong Cassidy, Paladin and the Cisco Kid

62. Lassie, Rin-Tin-Tin and Bullet

63. Mr. Ed, My Friend Flicker and Fury

64. Lloyd Bridges

65. The Peanut Gallery

66. Buffalo Bob Smith, Clarabell the Clown, Flubadub, Chief Thunderdud, Phenias T. Bluster, Cap'n Scuttlebutt, Trapper Pierre, Ranger Bob, Princes Summerfall Winterspring, Princess Gina Runningwater, Bison Bill, Sandra the Witch, J. Cornelius Cobb, and of course, Howdy Doody

67. 1947 to 1960

68. Algebra and Petie

69. Kennedy the Cop

70. Chubby and Joe (remember their boxing match?)

71. The high-sign – they'd put a hand under their chins, palm down, and wave

72. Norman, and Chubsie-Ubsie

73. Mrs. McGillicudy, Miss Crabtree and Miss Wilson

74. Mrs. McGillicudy was the only one never seen

75. Annette, Cubby, Sharon, Bobby, Lonnie, Doreen, Tommy and Karen

76. Mouseketeers

77. Who's the leader of the club that's made for you and me, M-I-C, K-E-Y, M-O-U-S-E! Mickey Mouse, Donald Duck. Forever let us hold our banner high, high, HIGH. Come along and sing our song, and join our jamboree. M-I-C, K-E-Y, M-O-U-S-E!

78. Minnie Mouse

79. Bugs Bunny, Daffy Duck, Elmer Fudd, Porky Pig, Sylvester, Tweety Bird, Foghorn-Leghorn, Henry Hawk, Barnyard Dawg, Wile E. Coyote, The Road Runner, Yosemite Sam, Beeky Buzzard, Gossamer

80. Heckle and Jeckle

81. Adam West

82. Burt Ward

83. Alan Napier

84. Cat Woman, Joker, Mr. Freeze, The Penguin, The Riddler, King Tut, Egghead, Mad Hatter, Louie the Lilac, Shame, Queen of the Cossacks, Queen of Diamonds

85.   Clark Kent

86.   Clark Kent, Lois Lane, Jimmy Olsen, Perry White

87.   "Great Caesar's ghost!

88.   The Daily Planet

89.   Inspector Henderson

90.   **Narrator:** Faster than a speeding bullet
       More powerful than a locomotive
       Able to leap tall buildings in a single bound
       Man 1: Look! Up in the sky! It's a bird!
       Woman: It's a plane!
       Man 2: It's Superman!
       Narrator: Yes, it's Superman
       Strange visitor from another planet who came to Earth with powers
       and abilities far beyond those of mortal men
       Superman, who can change the course of mighty rivers,
       Bend steel in his bare hands
       And who, disguised as Clark Kent
       Mild-mannered reporter for a great metropolitan newspaper
       Fights a never-ending battle for truth, justice and the American way!
       And now another exciting episode in the adventures of Superman!

91.   The Cleavers

92.   Eddy Haskell

93.   Grant Street Elementary

94.   Miss Landers

95.   Cowlick in his hair, over-alls, and a striped shirt

96.   Alfalfa from the Little Rascals/Our Gang

97.   Mr. Wilson

98.   Midnight the cat, Squeaky the mouse and Froggy the Gremlin, a frog

99.   Andy Devine

100.   "You've got a gang
       I've got a gang

Everybody's got to have a gang
But there's just one kind of gang for me
ANDY'S GANG!!!!!"

101. The Merry Mailman was Ray Heatherton; the cop was Officer Joe Bolton; The Sailor was Captain Jack McCarthy

102. Dead End Kids (which did *not* start out as a comedy)

103. Terrence Aloysius "Slip" Mahoney, Horace Debussy "Sach" Jones, Bobby Jordan, William "Whitey" Benedict, Gabriel Dell, Billy Halop and Bernard Punsly

104. Louie Dumbrowski

105. King Fish, Lightnin, Algonquin J. Calhoun and Saphire

106. Mystic Knights of the Sea

107. King Fish to Saphire

108. Mr. Fields

109. Mike the Cop

110. Stinky

111. Bingo

112. Bachagalup

113. Hilary

114. Ralph and Alice Kramden, and Ed and Trixie Norton

115. Bus driver

116. Ed Norton

117. 328 Chauncy Street, it's in Bushwick, not in Bensonhurst

118. Racoon Lodge

119. William Bendix and Jackie Gleason

120. Jedd, Granny, Jethro and Ellie Mae

121. Milburn Drysdale

122. Come and listen to my story 'Bout a man named Jed
A poor mountaineer, Barely kept his family fed
And then one day He was shootin' at some food
And up through the ground came a-bubblin' crude
Oil that is, black gold, Texas tea
Next thing you know ol' Jed's a millionaire
Kinfolk said, "Jed, 'Move away from there!'"
"'Said Californee is the place you oughta be'"
So they loaded up their truck and they moved to Beverly, Hills that is
Swimming pools, movie stars

123. Bugtussle, Tennessee

124. Gale Storm

125. Charles Farrell

126. Freddie Wilson

127. Eve Aren

128. The Mothers-In-Law

129. High school English teacher

130. Anne Jeffreys as Marion Kerby, Robert Sterling as George Kerby, Leo G. Carroll as Cosmo Topper, Lee Patrick as Henrietta Topper and Buck as Neil the dog

131. Cary Grant as George Kerby, Constance Bennett as Marion Kerby, Roland Young as Cosmo Topper and Billie Burke as Clara Topper

132. Dwayne Hickman

133. Maynard G. Krebs

134. Bob Denver

135. A beatnik

136. Gilligan's Island and the Good Guys

137. Grand Pappy Amos, Luke, Kate, Hassie and Little Luke

138. Peppino

139. Want you to meet the family, known as The Real McCoys
That's Grand Pappy Amos, the head of the clan,

He roars like a lion, but he's gentle as a lamb
And now here's Luke, who beams with joy since he made Kate
Missus Luke McCoy
From West Virginee they came to stay in sunny Californ-i-ay
Ol Grand Pappy Amos and the girls and the boys of the family known
as the Real McCoys

140. Oliver Wendel Douglas and Lisa Douglas, Mr. Haney, Eb Dawson, Hank Kimball, Sam Drucker, Doris Ziffel, Arnold Ziffel (the pig), Ralph and Alf Monroe

141. Green Acres is the place to be
Farm livin' is the life for me
Land spreadin' out so far and wide
Keep Manhattan, just give me that countryside

New York is where I'd rather stay. I get allergic smelling hay
I just adore a penthouse view
Dah-ling, I love you but give me Park Avenue

...The chores

...The stores

...Fresh air

...Times Square

You are my wife

Goodbye, city life

Green Acres we are there

142. Fred MacMurry

143. William Frawley, who played Uncle Bub on My Three Sons and as Fred Mertz on I Love Lucy

144. Tramp

145. Mike, Ernie, Robbie and then they adopted Chip when Mike married

his fiancé and was written off the show

146.   Desilu

147.   Band leader

148.   Ba-Ba-Loo

149.   Ethel and Fred Mertz

150.   623 68th Street, New York City (Manhattan)

151.   Herman, Lilly, Grandpa, Eddie and Marilyn

152.   1313 Mocking Bird Lane

153.   A pie in the face at the end of the Lunch With Soupy Sales show

154.   "Soupy told his viewers (most were children) to tiptoe into their sleeping parents' bedrooms and remove those "funny green pieces of paper with pictures of U.S. Presidents" from their parents' pants and pocketbooks. "Put them in an envelope and mail them to me." A few days later, envelopes with money started coming in the mail; Soupy said the total amount received was in the thousands of dollars, but that much of it was play money. Sales said he was joking and that whatever real money was received would be donated to charity, but as parents' complaints increased, WNEW suspended Sales for two weeks."
https://en.wikipedia.org/wiki/Soupy_Sales

155.   White Fang, Blacktooth, Pookie the Lion and Hippy the Hippo

156.   The Mouse

157.   Barbara Eden

158.   Major Antony Nelson, played by Larry Hagman

159.   Broderick Crawford

160.   Lee Marvin

161.   Starring Efrem Zimbalist Jr., Roger Smith, Richard Long and Edd Byrnes

162.   "Kookie, Kookie (Lend Me Your Comb)"

163. Jack Webb as Joe Friday

164. Ben Alexander as Officer Frank Smith and Harry Morgan as Officer Bill Gannon

165. Ladies and gentlemen, the story you are about to see is true. The names have been changed to protect the innocent.

166. Mark IV being chiseled into stone with a hammer hitting the chisel

167. David Jansen as Dr. Richard Kimball

168. Lt. Gerard

169. Roger Moore

170. James Bond

171. Craig Stevens

172. Robert Blake

173. The Little Rascals/Our Gang, known then as Michael James Gubitosi

174. Peggy Lipton, Clarence Williams III, Michael Cole

175. Julie Barnes, Linc Hayes, Pete Cochran

176. Captain Adam Greer

177. Ed Sullivan, Red Skelton, Your Show of Shows, Laugh In, Dean Martin, Smothers Brothers, Carol Burnet, Jackie Gleason Show, Sonny and Cher (these are the ones we remember; you might remember these and/or others)

178. Where the Action Is, Shindig, Hullabalu, American Bandstand, Soul Train, Midnight Special

179. Steve Martin

180. Paul Wintchell, Sherri Lewis, Edgar Bergen and Fran Allison

181. Paul Wintchell had Jerry Mahoney and Knucklehead Smith, Sherri Lewis had Lambchop and Charlie Horse, Edgar Bergen had Charlie McCarthy, Fran Allison had Kukla and Ollie

182. Saturday Night Fever, Lords of Flatbush, The Gang That Couldn't Shoot Straight, Do the Right Thing, Moonstruck, French Connection,

The Warriors, Crooklyn, Dog Day Afternoon, Coming To America, Ghost

183. Yoddles, Ring Dings, Yankee Doodles, Funny Bones, Devil Dogs, Drake's Fruit Pies, Drake's Coffee Cakes, Drake's Cream Filled Cupcakes – nothing better than ice-cold milk to wash them down, *but not coffee milk!*

184. Viceroy, Pall Mall, Old Gold, L&M, Winston, Demorier, Tareyton, Old Gold, Dunhill, Kent, Lucky Strike, Chesterfield, Merrit, Phillip Morris

185. Tareyton

186. Camel

187. Comet

188. Lassie and Lost in Space she played mother roles. She also portrayed Dr. Janet Craig on the CBS television sitcom Petticoat Junction

189. His major roles included Pete Porter in both December Bride and Pete and Gladys; Officer Bill Gannon on Dragnet; Amos Coogan on Hec Ramsey; and his starring role as Colonel Sherman T. Potter in M*A*S*H

190. "You wonder where the yellow went when you brush your teeth with Pepsodent."

191. Miller High Life

192. Shaeffer, is the, one beer to have, when you're having more than one
Shaeffer pleasure doesn't fade even when your thirst is done
The most rewarding flavor in this man's world, for people who are having fun
Shaeffer, is the, one beer to have, when you're having more than one

Schlitz is a dry beer, a hearty beer, a mellow beer, blended into one beer
A bright, light, fun beer. Schlitz, one beautiful beer

What'll you have? Pabst Blue Ribbon
What'll you have? Pabst Blue Ribbon
What'll you have? Pabst Blue Ribbon Pabst Blue Ribbon beer

193. N-E-S-T-L-E-S, Nestles makes the very best, Cho o o o-colate!

194.   A dog

195.   Mr. Clean will get rid of dirt and grime and grease in just a minute
Mr. Clean will clean your whole house and everything that's in it
Mr. Clean, Mr. Clean, Mr. Clean

196.   Once upon a time, there was an engineer
Choo-Choo Charlie was his name we hear
He had an engine, and he sure had fun
He used Good N Plenty to make his train run
Charlie says, "Love my Good N Plenty"
Charlie says, "Really rings a bell"
Charlie says, "Love my Good N Plenty"
"Don't know any other candy that I love so well"

197.   It's B-O, N-O, M-O
Bonomo's!
It's O O O
Bonomo's
Candy

198.   Bucky Beaver
Brusha-brusha-brusha
Here's the new Ipana
With the brand-new flavor
It's dandy for your teeth

199.   Brylcreem

200.   V7

201.   VO5 (there may have been a men's line, but it was mostly marketed towards women)

202.   "Chunky! What a chunk of chocolate!" Arnold Stang

203.   Bonomo's Turkish Taffy
Laffy Taffy
Ice Cubes (they were all chocolate)
Mary Janes
Candy corn
Reeds Butterscotch
Green Gene wax Lips
Nik-L-Nip – wax candies with juice inside them; some were bottle-

shaped or straws
Candy cigarettes – Round-Up and Target, among others
Gum cigars
Candy Buttons, they were candy dots on paper – and who didn't
sometimes eat the paper too!

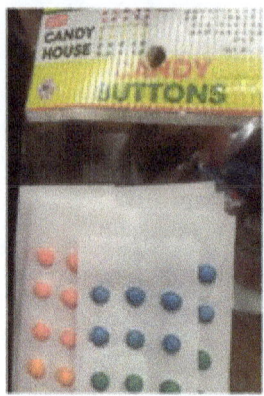

Dots

Junior Mints
Charleston Chew
Sugar Daddy
Good-N-Plenty
Mike-And-Ike
Chicklets
Reeces Peanut Butter Cups
Chunky
Snow Caps
Milk Duds
Bazooka Bubble Gum
Double Mint gum
Juicy Fruit

Pixie Stix -- straws with flavored sugar powder
Chuckles
Ring Pop
Wonka Bottle Caps
Candy Necklace
Lemonhead
Chocolate coins – the wrappers were foil and the chocolate was in the shape of different coins, complete with some head like a president
Red Hots
Razzles
Now And Laters
Gold Nuggets Bubble Gum
Smarties
Pez
Blow-Pops
Tootsie Rolls
Tootsie Pops
Sweet Tarts
Pop Rocks
Charms
Fruit Stripes
Mallo Cups
Swedish Fish
Slo Pokes
Astro Pops
Clark Bar
Baby Ruth
Hershey's
Mars Bars
Snickers
Milky Way
Oh Henry!
Power House
3 Musketeers
Marpro Yum Yum Candy Cones – and yes! They were fat-free!!
Goobers and Raisinets
M&Ms

204.   Chock Full O Nuts is that he-eh-eh-eh-venly coffee
        He-eh-eh-venly coffee
        He-eh-eh-venly coffee

Chock Full Of Nuts is that He-eh-eh-venly coffee
He-eh-eh-venly coffee
Better tasting coffee, a millionaire's money can't buy

205.   G and D was for Gambarelli & Davitto, nice Italian name! The was on TV with an attractive woman standing with a glass of what was supposed to be G&D Vermouth and she'd purr, "Mmmm. New York loves, G&D Vermouth."

206.   An owl

207.   Groucho Marx

208.   John Daly

209.   Julius La Rosa by Arthur Godfrey because Arthur Godfrey thought Julius La Rosa was getting bigger than he was

210.   Porky Pig, "a-the a-the-a-the-a, THAT'S ALL FOLKS!"

211.   Sunset, sunset, call hickory 64000
Hickory, hickory, hickory, hickory 64000

CONCLUSION

Ok, there you have it, I gave you what I got for the early years. Done by a kid from South-Brooklyn, which is really northern Brooklyn (*who knew*??), who lived a good life on the streets of Brooklyn. And who, till this day, at the age of 73, you still wanna hug or slap (correct Mrs. D. and Karen?). A man who has no regrets about the life that was handed to him ...or shoved in his face. I hope you enjoyed reading this book as much as I enjoyed writing it. Even though there were and are many trials and tribulations, some funny, some sad and some down-right ridiculous. They were all true, no fabrications here, not made up – you can't make this shit up (except for just one in the "STORIES" chapter that I left for you to figure out). It's always something! How's that Mark?

It was important to write this because it's about a bye-gone era, a long time ago, a time that will never be again; about people whose stories should be shared because they were loveable characters and many aren't here to tell it themselves. This is about people who were larger than life and who lived according to the rules they knew in the world they lived in back then, not today. These were real people with virtues and faults who just wanted to make it to the next day and have a little fun in the process. It's important to document these experiences, though some may be hard to believe or read about, but to give humanity to just some of the people I knew, who were otherwise not notable to anyone but maybe me. Just plain, regular folk. I hope I did them justice because I loved them all.

There's been a large change in Brooklyn and all over New York that brought in large numbers of new people, with new stories, from far-flung places. These new people have changed New York in so many ways. They've uncovered so many gems that us life-long Brooklynites may never have noticed or we took for granted – things that were right under our noses (and some of us had and still have some trombones – street slang for a big nose)! And of course, there are tensions between those who were born and raised here, and the people who moved here from someplace else. It's hard to believe that when we were growing up, Brooklyn was never a destination, it was the place you escaped from. There was a bigger world that was waiting, if you were fortunate enough to be able to get out. There were enough who never made it out, who had their beginning, middle and end, on the same street they were born on. Brooklyn is the biggest small town I know. You have to understand that many of us growing up were pigeon-holed by stereo-typical New York depictions like the Bowery Boys, gangster movies or that earnest, loveable lug from Brooklyn who gets killed in the WWII movies to show how savage the enemy was. And then there is that lovely, legendary Brooklyn accent, that made people judge us as not being too bright. You could be passed over for a job if you sounded too BQE, (Brooklyn-Queens Expressway-ish), or just plain too Brooklyn. Like this time when my dear friend Mick and I sat down to decompress after we broke up a fight at the East Village bar we worked at, and his girlfriend said to me, "You surprise me." I said, "Why's that?" She said, "Here I thought you were a witless brute, but you sat down and had a very civilized conversation..." Well, as we got older, we realized that coming from Brooklyn meant we had character (or knew a bunch of em), and grit. That we had a rich, colorful history and could be proud. The stories I've shared in this book are things I'm proud of, and I'm also fortunate to have known such a great bunch of people whose lives I can shine a small light on to give them some humanity.

Walking past places like the Brooklyn Museum, there are people going there to see the exhibits. We used to take our sleds to the hills behind it in the snow, to take sleigh rides. We NEVER thought about going in to see what was on display in the art world. When we walk past what used to be an empty lot in what used to be a dangerous neighborhood, there's a farmers market there now, with people milling about, not paying attention to their wallets... When we used to walk down some of those same streets, we looked over our shoulders in regular intervals to make sure we weren't being followed. Women clutched their handbags close to them and made sure the outer pockets of that pocketbook didn't have anything in it that was important in case someone tried to pick that pocket. We were hyper-aware of our surroundings because of the constant risk of being mugged or pick-pocketed. To now see the new gentry and the way they have the free mental space to enjoy their surroundings and to be able to focus on what they're actually doing, is mind-blowing for me because it ain't the Brooklyn I grew up in.

Anyway, I hope this put a good feeling in your heart, because being Italian, this is how we think, live and love. So, Gin Don! (Da end!!)

BUT STAY TUNED FOR BOOK 2!!

www.ingramcontent.com/pod-product-compliance
Lightning Source LLC
Chambersburg PA
CBHW061740120626
46550CB00005B/1845